MW01031446

The World
of
Nancy Kwan

The World of Nancy Kwan

A MEMOIR BY HOLLYWOOD'S ASIAN SUPERSTAR

NANCY KWAN
WITH DEBORAH DAVIS

LEGACY
LIT

New York Boston

Legacy Lit
Hachette Book Group
1290 Avenue of the Americas
New York, NY 10104
LegacyLitBooks.com
@LegacyLitBooks

First Edition: April 2025

Legacy Lit is an imprint of Grand Central Publishing. The Legacy Lit name and logo are registered trademarks of Hachette Book Group, Inc.

The publisher is not responsible for websites (or their content) that are not owned by the publisher.

The Hachette Speakers Bureau provides a wide range of authors for speaking events. To find out more, go to hachettespeakersbureau.com or email HachetteSpeakers@hbgusa.com.

Legacy Lit books may be purchased in bulk for business, educational, or promotional use. For information, please contact your local bookseller or the Hachette Book Group Special Markets Department at special.markets@hbgusa.com.

Print book interior design by Taylor Navis.

Library of Congress Control Number: 2024951268

ISBNs: 978-0-306-83427-1 (hardcover); 978-0-306-83429-5 (ebook)

Printed in Canada

MRQ-T

1 2025

To Stardust

I was asked if I would like to live my life over again. While writing my memoir, I relived my life. And what I learned from this is that nothing is permanent.

We are just passing through.

CONTENTS

CONTENTS

FOREWORD

Let me set the scene. It was sometime in the early 1990s. A gas station on a remote two-lane highway on the Bolivar Peninsula of the Gulf Coast of Texas. I was paying at the counter when a menacing-looking guy with a grizzled beard dressed in classic Hell's Angels attire stared at my credit card suspiciously. I started getting worried until he gruffly asked, "Kevin Kwan...you related to Nancy Kwan?"

I laughed in relief. "She's my cousin."

His face transformed from threatening to wonder. "Are you kiddin' me? Man, she was the woman of my dreams!"

I was suddenly transported back to my childhood in Singapore, where I had heard this same question asked of my parents too many times to remember. *Are you related to Nancy?* I suppose this is what happens when you are related to an icon. (Nancy is my second cousin thrice removed, to be precise.) Long before I ever met her or knew much about her, her name had always been part of my consciousness. Amongst my relatives, Nancy seemed to be some sort of standard bearer, as I recall overhearing comments like "She's not as beautiful as Nancy" or "She's not as good a dancer as Nancy." Other times, her name would be used to explain certain members of the family. "She went to school in London and dyed her hair purple. She's turned out to be one of the artsy ones—like Nancy."

I didn't understand what all this meant until one night when I was around eight or nine. There was great excitement in the house as the entire family gathered around the big television in my grandparents' bedroom to watch a movie that was being broadcast for the first time in years. As *Flower Drum Song* came on, I remember being surprised to see all these Asians on-screen speaking with American accents and behaving like Americans. Till this moment, I was only used to seeing other Asians in Hong Kong soap operas or martial arts films. About ten minutes into the film, a musical number unfolded in a fancy nightclub and this woman suddenly emerged from behind a cluster of fluttering fans singing "Fan Tan Fannie." "There's Nancy!," my grandfather beamed proudly. "She has the Kwan look," my aunt assessed. My jaw dropped. This was *the* Nancy Kwan I had heard so much about? All this time I had imagined some fusty old auntie with a beehive perm. This gorgeous, glamorous angel prancing around the stage was *related to me*? I was utterly transfixed, and that night I fell in love with her, just like millions of other people did decades earlier when she made her big screen debut in *The World of Suzie Wong*.

Back then, I was too young to appreciate what Nancy Kwan meant to others. Nancy didn't just belong to my family. In many ways, she was a bridge between East and West, the first Asian to become a global superstar. She was a leading lady who commanded top billing alongside Hollywood legends like William Holden, Glenn Ford, and Tony Curtis. Paparazzi chased her every move all over Europe. Elvis Presley begged her to star in his movie. Vidal Sassoon cut her hair into a daring bob, and it became an international sensation. She was on the cover of *Life* magazine. She was the first Asian woman to start her own film studio. She inspired a whole generation of Asian women in the 1960s to be bold and independent, to celebrate themselves. She made it cool to be Asian, and her success paved the way for another emerging actor to become a superstar—Bruce Lee. It's only fitting that six decades later Quentin Tarantino featured a scene of Nancy with Bruce Lee and Sharon Tate in his film *Once upon a Time in Hollywood*.

Nancy is one of the remaining links to that time, to Old Hollywood, to the last gasps of the studio system. While she recounts the famous stars she met, glittering Hollywood premieres, and fabulous pool parties, she also unflinchingly documents the jaw-dropping prejudices and hardships that she faced—alone—in that era. Being the first and only Asian in the room wasn't easy, but Nancy confronted each challenge with grace, shattering the stereotypes one by one. She not only survived, she triumphed.

Looking back, I think that watching *Flower Drum Song* that night with my family influenced me in ways I'm only beginning to understand now. Seeing Nancy on the big screen so early in my life left an indelible mark. This cool cousin showed me what was possible. She proved that I could be one of the artsy ones and pursue a creative life as well. She inspired me to celebrate my culture and write stories about the crazy antics of a family in Singapore. But as I said from the beginning, Nancy doesn't just belong to my family. I know she's inspired countless other people in other families around the world. In sharing this precious and important story now, she will continue to do so for generations to come.

Kevin Kwan

The World
of
Nancy Kwan

PROLOGUE

I t is fascinating to see the world getting smaller. Now more than ever the many cultures are merging as never before. How different it was when I was growing up. People were more intolerant of our culture. To be Eurasian at the time was more of a challenge in so many ways, whereas today we have evolved and have a better understanding of each other.

I have always been proud of who I am. I come from two cultures, my father was Chinese and my mother was English, and I always felt it gave me a better understanding of human nature. I would like to think of us as Citizens of the World, and if we learn to put aside our racial and religious prejudices, what a wonderful world it would be.

I wanted to be a ballet dancer, but somehow fate had other plans. I hung up my toe shoes and became an actress. That was many years ago, but I believe the past, the present, and the future are woven together in the fabric of destiny, with its intricate patterns of joy and sadness, love and loss. I've broken barriers, celebrated achievements, overcome disappointments, and survived tragedies, all part of my remarkable journey from Hong Kong to Hollywood and beyond. This is my story.

Nancy Kwan

CHAPTER 1

"East is east, and west is west, and never the twain shall meet," wrote Rudyard Kipling.

But the twain *did* meet when my father, Kwan Wing Hong, nicknamed "Hongkie," began an internship at a movie studio in London in 1936. Born and raised in Hong Kong, he was sent to boarding school in England at the tender age of eight and then studied at Cambridge. Several years later, when he graduated from the London School of Architecture, he decided to work at the studio with an eye toward designing one for his wealthy family in Hong Kong. He took his job on set very seriously. One day, he saw a young woman place her shoes on a chair. He told her it was a prop and ordered her to remove them immediately. Then he took a closer look: the woman was beautiful.

Marquita Scott was a model and aspiring actress working as an extra in the film. She grew up in Worthing, a seaside town in Sussex, England, known for its health spa, where people came to experience the restorative powers of seawater. Worthing also boasted one of England's first cinemas, The Dome, which opened in 1911. Marquita's ambition to move to London to become an actress may have been born in that very theater, where she watched the films of Madeleine Carroll and other young British stars. Their glamorous images beckoned, suggesting that beauty could take you far and make dreams come true.

Marquita moved to London, made the rounds of modeling agencies and casting offices, and ended up as an extra in a film. Even if her feet hurt, and she had to listen to an annoying young man tell her where she could and couldn't sit, she was one step closer to making her dreams a reality.

Blonde and fair of face, in that English rose way—*stunning*, actually—Marquita smiled at that annoying young man, instantly dispelling all thoughts of shoes, props, and rules. There was an immediate attraction between them that sparked romance, then marriage. My father sailed home to Hong Kong with the lovely Marquita as his bride, although a spurned suitor followed my mother to the ocean liner, begging her not to leave.

In Hong Kong, the newlyweds stayed with my grandfather, Kwan Chee Woh, who had a storied life. When I look back on my ancestors, I realize that they *all* had remarkable histories. They were born in small villages in China, where they experienced the hardships of poverty. Despite their humble beginnings, they managed to build extraordinary lives filled with accomplishment, public service, and, in some cases, incredible wealth.

My grandfather had fourteen siblings. His father, my great-grandfather Kwan Yuen Cheung, was born in China in 1832, and at a young age, he moved to Hong Kong to work for the London Missionary Society. He went on to become the first Western-trained dentist in Hong Kong, and through the missionary network, he met Lai Amui.

Lai Amui, my great-grandmother, was tragically separated from her parents during the Taiping rebellion and was found— literally on their doorstep—by a British couple, a police officer and his wife living in Canton, who raised her and enrolled her in the local missionary-run girls' school. After the introduction to my great-grandfather, she moved from Canton to Hong Kong to be his wife and became the first Western-trained nurse in the city.

The Kwans were devout Christians who lived by a family creed. "Trust in the God of Christianity, wherever and whenever, help those who are less fortunate. Study medicine and engineering and contribute to society and mankind." They were also studious and ambitious.

My great-uncle Kwan King Leung, number seven son, attended the Hong Kong College of Medicine, where one of his closest friends was a young man who grew up to be Dr. Sun Yat-Sen. They spent so much time together, even forming a discussion group they called "the four bandits," that my great-grandmother considered Sun Yat-Sen her godson.

The two men found themselves on the opposite side of history, though, when my great-uncle became the physician to the Empress Dowager of China. With her appointee Emperor Puyi, they were the last representatives of the Manchu, or the Qing Dynasty. Meanwhile, his friend Dr. Sun Yat-Sen became a political philosopher and revolutionary. He was instrumental in overthrowing the Empress Dowager and the Qing Dynasty, and in 1911 went on to become the first provisional president of the Republic of China and the first leader of the Nationalist Party of China.

I don't know if Great-uncle Kwan King Leung's friendship with Dr. Sun Yat-Sen endured, but I think it is extraordinary that the man who is considered the father of modern China spent his formative years in the Kwan household.

Kwan King Chung, number nine son, went on to become the great-great-grandfather of Kevin Kwan, author of the internationally bestselling *Crazy Rich Asians* trilogy, books inspired by the opulent world he experienced while growing up in Singapore.

My own grandfather Kwan Chee Woh, number thirteen son, was educated at Cambridge in England and Cornell University in America. A brilliant mineralogist, he went to work for a wealthy tin magnate named Loke Yew, whose story is also connected to mine.

Like the Kwans, Loke Yew was born in China. He moved to Singapore and spent four years saving the equivalent of ninety-nine dollars, which he invested in businesses that grew into a vast empire of Malaysian tin mines.

Loke Yew was so impressed by Chee Woh that he placed him in charge of his mines and, most importantly, arranged for him to marry his daughter, Juliann Loke. The couple produced a son— my father, Kwan Wing Hong—but the marriage didn't work out. My grandmother stayed with her family in Malaysia while my grandfather took his young son to Hong Kong.

There, Chee Woh invested in real estate in Kowloon Tong, an affluent part of the city. A devout Christian, he built Christ Church for his fellow residents and established a large household for his extended family, my parent's first home when they arrived as newlyweds in Hong Kong.

A cousin told me our relatives were excited to have my foreign mother join the family. I wonder if they appreciated her Western beauty. My mother could converse with my grandfather and my great aunt, who spoke English, and the young couple was showered with wedding presents, including silver, silk, and porcelain treasures from the Imperial Court, which Great-uncle Kwan King Leung acquired when he was the Empress Dowager's physician.

Eventually, my father demonstrated his architectural talent by building their first home, an Art Deco house on Homantin Hill, one of Hong Kong's most desirable neighborhoods.

Still, the reality of Hong Kong was probably very different from what my mother imagined. It must have been difficult for her to adjust to being a member of a traditional Chinese family. And, although the city had a mixed population of Chinese and British residents, I doubt the world outside their home was welcoming to an interracial couple: Hong Kong was a British colony with a complicated history and a confusion of identities that persists to this day.

In the early nineteenth century, Hong Kong was a small and sparsely populated coastal settlement in China, inhabited by fishermen who were ruled by the Qing Dynasty. The island's natural harbor made it a convenient stopping place for British trading ships (and ones from other Western countries) sailing to and from Southeast Asia.

These merchants were unhappy about their commercial dealings with China because they were at the wrong end of a trade imbalance. There was a high demand for Chinese imports such as tea, silk, and porcelain in European countries, but the Chinese were less interested in Western goods. Money went into China but did not come out, creating a trade deficit. The British East India Company solved the problem by licensing private traders to operate a market guaranteed to become a booming business: the opium trade.

Opium was used for medicinal purposes in China but not for recreation until these foreign merchant ships provided a steady supply—and collected hefty payments in gold and silver. Predictably, and as planned, a large percentage of the Chinese population became addicted to the drug. When the emperor saw the negative effect that opium addiction had on his country, he tried to ban it and destroyed a large shipment, causing British merchants to lose a fortune. They cried foul, and the first of two "Opium Wars" ensued in 1839. England was a stronger military power than China and easily won the war, then demanded more favorable trade terms, reparations, and control of Hong Kong, which, after the Treaty of Nanking, became a British Crown colony in perpetuity.

A second Opium War broke out in 1856 when a British-French alliance fought to have opium legalized in China. The foreigners won again, claiming Hong Kong's Kowloon Peninsula as part of their colony.

In June 1898, another treaty was negotiated allowing Britain to lease additional Hong Kong territories for the next ninety-nine years.

China took this opportunity to protest the unfair treaties the country had been forced to accept during the "Century of Humiliation," as they called their inequitable history with the West. They negotiated the more favorable Sino-British Joint Declaration, which arranged for ownership of Hong Kong and its territories to be transferred back to China in 1997.

When the British took over Hong Kong, they set out to remake the city in their image, which was usually the case with colonies. They built a modern infrastructure, including roads, railways, and port facilities, established an effective civil service, and introduced a legal system that included trial by jury, improvements that positioned Hong Kong to become a major international financial center and trading hub.

But the British also replicated the social divisions they'd known in their own country, establishing a caste system for the Chinese, who were excluded from high-level jobs, social clubs, and white-only neighborhoods.

On the other side, the Chinese, who had their own economic and social hierarchy, and whose culture was older and indigenous, had deep-rooted prejudices about socializing with foreigners.

My mother was caught between these two "never the twain shall meet" worlds, and though she must have overcome challenging situations in the past (her career as an aspiring actress was a bold choice for a woman back then), I'm certain she had trouble finding her place in Hong Kong.

As it turned out, assimilation and acceptance weren't her biggest problems. She preferred attention and excitement over domesticity, so she was unprepared for the less glamorous role of wife and then mother when my brother, Kwan Ka Keung, known as KK, was born a little over a year after my parents married.

I followed eighteen months later, in 1939, and was named Kwan Ka Shen. My mother's mother, Granny May, traveled from far-off England on a three-month journey by ship to be present at my birth. She was a warm and steadying presence, but when my father realized that war in Europe was imminent, he urged Granny to return to her family before it would be impossible to travel.

After she went home, everything fell apart, and the unthinkable happened. Sometime between 1939 and 1941, when I was still a baby, my mother left us. She packed her things and abandoned her husband and children to move to Shanghai. Was she overwhelmed by motherhood? Had she realized she would be better off without children because she was more interested in caring for herself? Did she long for freedom and a more exciting life in Shanghai, the city known as the Paris of the Orient? I don't know because my father never spoke of her. It was as if she had never existed. I was too young to remember her presence, but her absence would always be with me.

The domestic drama in our home was overshadowed by the terrible threat of war with Japan. Even before the start of World War II, Japanese attacks on China were brutal, including the infamous Nanjing Massacre, or Rape of Nanking, in 1937, when three hundred thousand civilians and unarmed soldiers were murdered and tens of thousands of women were sexually assaulted. While Hitler invaded Europe, Japan took advantage of the ensuing global chaos to advance its mission to purge Asia of the influences of the West and seize control of China.

On December 7, 1941, Japan bombed an American naval base at Pearl Harbor in Honolulu. Eight hours later, Japan also attacked Hong Kong. The British were unable to defend the colony because military resources were strained at home. A small battalion of the Royal Rifles of Canada was deployed to fight alongside a Hong Kong volunteer unit, but they were easily defeated by the Japanese army. Hong Kong surrendered to Japan on Christmas Day, "Black Christmas," as it was later called.

The Japanese army moved into Hong Kong with a harsh mandate—to subjugate, plunder, rape, and destroy. Our very survival was at stake, so my father had to act quickly to save his young family. He arranged transport on a ship to Macao, then had to figure out how to slip past the Japanese checkpoint, where soldiers stopped everyone who had children and baggage to prevent them from leaving. Daddy decided to bluff his way through by pretending to be an imperious government official traveling with his entourage—a young Chinese woman we knew as

"Aunty Nan" and his cook. He hid my brother and me in woven baskets that hung from a pole on our cook's shoulders.

We made it to Macao, which was overrun with refugees. My father doubted we'd be able to survive there, so he found a junk to carry us from Macao to the Chinese mainland. It was a nine-hour crossing in total darkness so that we could evade Japanese patrol boats. I'm told I cried the whole way. On shore, my father used the same ruse to clear another tense checkpoint. Knowing that getting caught would mean execution, he hired two sedan chairs and several porters to impress the soldiers, hoping they would assume he was wealthy and important and let him pass.

His ruse worked. We cleared the checkpoint and traveled 160 miles on foot, finally arriving in a rural area in Free China, where life presented endless threats. The conditions were so unsanitary that disease was everywhere, and even though I was only four years old, I remember being so sick that I almost died. I never knew the name of my illness. There were no Western doctors where we lived, so Aunty Nan sent for an herbalist, who collected healing plants from the forest and boiled them into a medicinal brew. I drank it and recovered.

My father warned me never to enter the outhouse, a makeshift assemblage of wooden planks used strictly by the adults. I was a curious child and found a way to sneak inside. I slipped on a wet plank and fell into the hole, screaming as I tried to get out. Thankfully, my father appeared and yanked me out of the stinking mess. Even after a thorough scrubbing, I could still smell the stench on me for days.

Time passed, but the occasional joy of playing in the hills with my brother couldn't dispel the ache in my empty stomach, which rarely went away. The Maryknoll priests in the area kept an eye on us and gave us milk and bits of food—if we were lucky, chocolate and cookies—but never enough to keep us from feeling hungry.

If the physical hardships were difficult to bear, the constant threat of an enemy attack was worse. I will never forget the piercing sound of sirens warning us to take cover. They signaled the approach of Japanese bombers in the skies over the village. We ran as fast as we could, sheltering in the nearby caves until the danger passed. To this day, the sound of sirens makes the hair on my arms stand up, a reminder of the terror I experienced as a child.

At some point, while we were in China, my father married Aunty Nan, who became our stepmother. KK and I weren't told about the change in her status—it just happened. In our culture, adults never explained their actions to their children. Our family grew to include my half-sister, Betty.

I was confused when my father disappeared for long periods, leaving us in the care of Aunty Nan. He always returned and was so happy to see us. One day, he was surprised to find me riding on the back of a water buffalo in a rice paddy. He didn't speak about the purpose of his trips until years later when I was old enough to understand. Then, I learned he was an agent with the BAAG, the British Army Aid Group. Daddy and two of his friends were recruited by the British when the Japanese invaded Hong Kong, but shortly after they started working undercover, one of his friends, Jimmy Caldwell, was captured and beheaded. Knowing how dangerous the assignment was, my father agreed to do "Evasion and Evacuation work," helping soldiers who'd fallen behind enemy lines to escape from the Japanese. His code name was "DOMUS."

He didn't like to talk about the war, but he did tell us one story about an American plane the Japanese shot down in China. Daddy rushed to the crash site and found the pilot shaking with fear, pointing a gun at him because he assumed his Asian rescuer was the enemy. In his best British accent, my father convinced the pilot he was a friend who would take him somewhere safe—a challenge even in broad daylight during those dangerous times—until he had the ingenious idea of hiding the pilot in a Nanning brothel for a few days, a clever way to elude the Japanese.

My father was an architect, not a military man, yet he risked his life in desperate situations to protect his country and its allies. His British comrades greatly appreciated his bravery throughout the war and praised him for his "initiative of a high order and utmost devotion to duty."

He also worked with the Flying Tigers, the American pilots who volunteered to help the China Air Force fight the Japanese. They were so grateful for his help that they sent my brother one of their signature jackets. They also gave us a parachute, and Aunty Nan used the fabric to make me a dress.

I'm sorry we didn't speak more about my father's wartime experiences when he was alive. So much of that time is lost to me because I was so young, but I'm not surprised that Daddy was quietly heroic. He did not seek praise for his courage; he did what he believed was right.

While we were hiding in China, our relatives faced perilous times in Hong Kong. The city was destroyed during the Japanese occupation; families were separated and endured disease, famine, and execution, usually by public beheading or firing squad. Some corpses were dumped in the river, others were left in the streets. Men were arrested and sent to POW and labor camps while women of all ages were taken from their homes and forced into sexual slavery. Called "comfort women," they had to service the Japanese soldiers. The people who escaped death or captivity still had to contend with the daily hell of finding food for survival. Many starved to death. These atrocities sound as if they might have happened in medieval times, not in a cosmopolitan city in the twentieth century.

People were afraid to leave their homes, and everyone who stayed in Hong Kong faced life-or-death situations. Some were more fortunate than others. Soldiers forced their way into my grandfather's house and ordered my aunts and cousins to remain silent and not look at them as they searched the downstairs area. Then they went upstairs, where they found my grandfather, who was ill and confined to his bed, and my great-aunt. A Japanese officer noticed she was reading a book and asked what it was. When she told him she was reading the Bible, he said, "My grandmother also reads the Bible."

That moment of connection transcended the barriers war had placed between them. The officer promised the family they could live upstairs while the soldiers took over the first floor. Only their cook was allowed to venture downstairs to use the kitchen. They were captives, but the officer's protection gave them a measure of safety. My grandfather's beloved Christ Church was turned into a stable for the Japanese army's horses.

The war ended soon after the United States dropped atomic bombs on Hiroshima and Nagasaki. The Japanese surrendered in September 1945, and the occupation of Hong Kong, which had lasted three years and eight months, was over.

We returned to Hong Kong and discovered that we had to stay with my grandfather in Kowloon Tong because the Japanese had turned our beautiful home into a barracks, and it was in terrible shape. In ways too complicated for me to understand—then or now—the Kwans managed to safeguard their money during the war, so we could rebuild what we had lost.

We saw the effects of war everywhere. So many people had perished between 1941 and 1945. I was too young to remember what Hong Kong looked like before the occupation, but I learned that parts of the city were unrecognizable. I saw groups of dazed Japanese soldiers waiting to be sent to their next destination. High-ranking Japanese officers had been arrested, but demilitarization was a slower process for the troops they left behind.

I remember playing outside in our garden and coming across some soldiers, perhaps the same ones who had lived in our house during the occupation, who were waiting to be shipped out. One of the men motioned to me, mimicking smoking. Could I get him a cigarette? I ran into the house, took a cigarette from my father's pack of Lucky Strikes, and brought it back to him, thrilled by my daring. It never occurred to me that helping the enemy might be the wrong thing to do.

Eventually, we resumed our lives. I felt safe and stopped listening for sirens. We moved into our house, dined on bountiful meals instead of rations, went to school, and played with friends.

My family (even my Cambridge-educated father) loved reading comic books, and when I was seven or eight years old, I figured out how to turn our pastime into a business. One day, while strolling through the street market, I spotted four men sitting at a stall reading *The Monkey King*, a classic Chinese novel written during the Ming Dynasty. The men didn't own the book; they rented it from the vendor, who charged them for each chapter. I had an idea!

I went to see my friend Pat Wong to explain my business plan. We could set up a stand and charge people ten cents to read our comics, I said. I needed her as my partner because she lived in an apartment building that had much more foot traffic than my secluded house. Pat and I laid out the comic books and waited for customers. On the first day, we had one reader. On the second day, we had three, including a girl who took so long to read the comic that I got bored watching her, and a boy who didn't like what he read and demanded a refund. We almost came to blows when we refused to give it to him. By day three, business boomed: four customers stopped by, but one had no money. That's when I decided to close our retail operation. I didn't have the patience to stick with my idea.

As it turned out, comic books had a much greater impact on my life after my failed start-up. I always looked forward to reading "Nancy," the American comic about a mischievous young girl with that name. I announced I wanted to be called "Nancy" instead of Ka Shen. It was a time of new beginnings, and in that spirit, I became Nancy Kwan.

CHAPTER 2

After so many years of missed holidays during wartime, we looked forward to celebrating with our relatives. My favorite was the Chinese New Year. There was always a sense of excitement when our amahs, the women who worked for the family, busily cleaned and prepared special foods like turnip cake and sticky rice pudding for the four-day celebration. The elaborate candy box in the living room was filled with baked seeds, nuts, and sweets, and we dressed in new clothes and shoes.

On New Year's Eve, the entire family visited the flower market to purchase peach blossoms, plum blossoms, orchids, and lucky bamboo for the house, setting the stage for the festivities ahead. Every flower had a meaning and was displayed to symbolize prosperity or success in the New Year. "Gung Hay Fat Choy (Good health and good fortune)!" we excitedly wished each other on New Year's Day as we were given bright red packets filled with money. The amahs were happy, too, because they received a bonus to commemorate the holiday.

We gathered at grandfather's house, where many more red packets came our way, and thrilled to the sound of firecrackers as they lit up the garden to ward off evil spirits. We were always eager to visit Uncle Lee and his family at their mansion on the

Hong Kong side. We weren't related to him by blood, but we called all Daddy's friends "uncle" and "aunty."

Uncle Lee, a wealthy man who owned banks in Hong Kong, was particularly colorful because he maintained a wife and four mistresses. All five stood at the door to greet us, dressed beautifully in silk Chinese gowns. I noticed they all wore the same gold watch. Later, I heard Aunty Nan tell a friend that having a wife and four mistresses must be very expensive. "Wait till they all ask for a diamond ring," she laughed, acknowledging that he *had* to keep them happy, or he wouldn't have enough mahjong legs (players) for his game. Uncle Lee, who was generous to us, too, distributed fat red packets to the children, and his amahs passed around colorful candy boxes, urging us to help ourselves. I stuffed my pockets and always ended up with a stomachache. But that didn't stop me from spending the holiday money I stored in my piggy bank on candy and more candy.

While driving to my grandfather's house one day, I noticed an impressive building. My father told me it was the Maryknoll Convent School, run by nuns, and I decided I had to go there. It turned out to be the perfect school for me. As I got older, I was more conscious of being Eurasian, the term used to describe the progeny of mixed marriages. The freckles I inherited from my mother attracted a lot of attention on the streets of Hong Kong. Strangers came up to me and stared at my face. The bold ones asked if the freckles were pimples. The *rude* ones called me a half-caste. Either way, I was made to feel different, like an outsider.

But at Maryknoll, many of my classmates were Eurasian, just like me, so I didn't feel out of place. I was a diligent student and appreciated the school's order, tranquility, and predictable routines. We wore white uniforms in the summer and blue in the winter, and our studies and activities were overseen by nuns who were kind and attentive. They were so impressive that I told my father *I* wanted to be a nun when I grew up. He wisely said, "Why don't you wait to think about that? When you're older, you can decide for yourself," and I promptly forgot about it.

My friends and I were very curious about the voluminous habits the nuns wore to cover their bodies. We tried to spy on them when they swam in their pool, hoping to see an inch of human flesh underneath all that cloth, but our efforts were thwarted, and we never saw anything. They remained mysterious figures, almost saintlike in their dedication to God and us.

The nuns were so attentive that they immediately questioned me when I showed up at school with red welts on my legs. I made up a story about falling and getting scratched, but they suspected something else had caused the ugly marks—and they were correct.

I was too ashamed to tell them my stepmother Aunty Nan beat my legs with a bamboo feather duster. I can't remember what I did to provoke her on that particular day, or if I did anything at all. I was a spirited child, but no more so than other children, and these beatings were how she dealt with me. Now, I wonder if my very existence—my freckled face, a constant reminder of my father's ill-fated first marriage to his beautiful, rebellious English wife—made my stepmother want to punish me, her rival's daughter. As close as I was to my father, I never had that bond with Aunty Nan.

The nuns took my predicament very seriously and immediately called on my parents. I was shocked to see my favorite nun, Sister Matthew Marie, and Mother Superior sitting with my stepmother in our living room. They wanted to speak to my father, but he was in Malaysia working on a construction project for the Shell Oil Company. Eventually, my father heard about the incident, and the feather duster beatings stopped, but the emotional distance between my stepmother and me remained.

Then came a surprise visit from Marquita, my long-lost mother. I heard or probably overheard that she was stranded in Shanghai during the war and had an affair with a Chinese man from San Francisco, but that he killed himself when the war ended. I don't know what happened to her after that.

One day, she appeared as suddenly as she'd disappeared. I was nine when I came home from school to find her sitting on the couch. It was as if I were seeing her for the first time. She was beautiful—blonde and statuesque, like a goddess. I took one look and ran out of the room. My brother visited with her, but I refused. In my mind, she was a stranger, or worse—the mother who abandoned me when I was a baby. I guess I must have suppressed a lot of emotions, but the situation was too complicated for a child to process, so it was easier for me to walk away and pretend it wasn't happening. She didn't make me feel the comfort of a maternal presence in my life.

Then when I was about ten, the whole family joined Daddy in North Borneo, now known as Sabah. He was still working for Shell, building temporary structures for company workers. I had no idea where Borneo was except that my stepmother, Aunty Nan, was from Jesselton (Kota Kinabalu), the capital of Sabah. She and her family were known as Hakka, an ethnic group concentrated in Southern China.

It was the first time I had ever been on a plane. My older brother, KK, and I excitedly pressed our noses to the window to get a bird's-eye view of Kowloon as it slowly disappeared into the ocean. I still remember feeling sick to my stomach, so nauseous that I started vomiting. I don't know how long it took to get to Sabah, it couldn't have been more than three or four hours, but I just wanted to get off the plane. When we landed, I told my father, "I'm staying with you. I am never getting on a plane again!"

We stayed in a bungalow that my father built. Behind the house was the mysterious jungle, with monkeys and colorful birds in the trees. "Don't go into the jungle," the adults warned because there were snakes, wild animals, and who knows what else. Our father's housekeeper told us a story about a man on his way home after having a few drinks—he stopped to take a pee by the side of the road, and a crocodile bit off his testicles! That was warning enough for us.

After I recovered from the flight from Hong Kong, Aunty Nan took us to visit her mother, our Pau-Pau (Cantonese for grand-mother from the wife's side), in the coastal area. Pau-Pau and her three youngest children lived in a stilt house, which was elevated to protect against flooding and vermin. They're usually built of bamboo and wood, with a thatched roof and wooden walls per-forated with windows and lattice. This one had two stories. The bedrooms were upstairs, where the children slept together on mats on the floor. Downstairs was a small area for cooking and a large table where we ate our meals. There was no sewer system, so raw sewage flowed directly into the sea.

We were so excited to be staying in such a primitive place. On our first night, as soon as the water retreated to its lowest level, we were each given a flashlight and a spear, and "Number Seven Uncle" taught us how to hunt for crabs by shining the torch over the muddy area until we spotted what looked like a pair of eyes. A crab! Then we'd aim the spear at the crab and catch it. They were delicious! At high tide, we'd sit on the platform attached to the back of the stilt house and fish for supper. Even the act of gathering food for meals was an adventure.

One predawn morning, I went with Aunty Nan, "Number Six Aunt," and her younger sister, "Number Eight Aunt," to search for durians, a fruit with a pungent scent. We waited patiently for the sound of the ripening durian as it hit the ground. I had never seen Aunty Nan so excited. The nasty odor led you to the durian before you saw it. The three sisters swooned over the stinky fruit, blissful as they devoured what smelled like cat feces to me! I tried one when I was older but never acquired a taste for them.

One day, Daddy packed the family onto a longboat and took us deep into the forbidden jungle to visit his friends. I had never seen so much life along a riverbank. As we moved slowly through the water, we spotted the ever-present monkeys and birds in the trees, crocodiles basking on the shore, and herds of pygmy elephants in the brush. Finally, we arrived at our destination, the longhouse, a narrow, covered veranda with doors on all sides. The entire village lived under one roof, with families making their homes in different rooms. My father introduced us to his friends, and we witnessed a beautiful Malay sunset. At night, we dined on a communal feast. After dinner, we were offered mats in the large room where everyone slept.

When we returned to Pau-Pau's house, Daddy gave us a warning. Aunty Nan and her family had been living in Malaysia for generations, so they were well aware of the practice of black magic in the country (which still exists in Malaysia today). Even though my father was an educated man and a Christian, he respected the practice of other religions and the power of the unknown. He had heard stories about people who were the victims of mysterious spells (in Cantonese—*Gong Tau*). Thinking it was better to be safe than sorry, he talked about the dangers of black magic and laid down the rules we had to follow during our visit.

Daddy told us not to go shopping in the marketplace alone— we had to be accompanied by an adult—and never buy anything ourselves, handle money, or accept gifts from the vendors.

Of course, we wanted to know why.

He explained that, with black magic, children were sometimes spirited away and never found again. After that, whenever I went shopping in the market, I secretly gave the evil eye to anyone who looked suspicious.

Sometimes spells were cast to exact vengeance. A few years after our trip to Borneo, Aunty Nan told us that Number Six Aunt, who had joined us on our expedition to hunt for durians, suffered a terrible death after a man she rejected used black magic on her: Supposedly, she vomited snakes and other reptiles until she collapsed and later died. I say *supposedly*, but she was taken to a hospital, and doctors were unable to save her because there was no medical explanation for her condition.

Most Asians are superstitious. I believe in spirits, ghosts, the supernatural, and karma. What a contradiction for a Christian and a Buddhist, but, like my father, I respect all religions and acknowledge that the universe holds many mysteries we will never fully understand.

Amazingly, we encountered this exotic place with its primordial landscape and enduring superstitions in *1949*, when the rest of the world, including Hong Kong, embraced modernity. It was like straddling parallel universes, with black magic on one side and emerging technology on the other. Post-war Hong Kong, still a British colony, was evolving from a sleepy fishing village to a bustling city, with an exploding population of refugees pouring in from Communist China to escape Mao Zedong and the Soviet-inspired People's Republic of China. They were everywhere, lined up in the streets, trying to find food and shelter.

We had all the modern conveniences, including television, and one night when I was seven or eight, I watched a program on our black-and-white set that made a deep impression on me and changed the course of my life. Margot Fonteyn danced in a filmed presentation of the Royal Ballet's production of *The Sleeping Beauty*, the company's first ballet when the Royal Opera House reopened after the war. I was spellbound and immediately asked my father if I could take ballet lessons. He thought it would be good for me and found Mrs. Reynolds and her daughter Babs, two Canadian ex-pats who ran a local ballet academy.

My first class was so exciting. *I love this. I'm going to do it*, I thought, as I stretched and imitated the movements my teachers demonstrated. I couldn't wait for my next lesson. I worked hard in class, danced around the house practicing my steps, and progressed to being *en pointe* in record time. I didn't mind long hours at the barre, sewing ribbons onto my ballet shoes, or wrapping my bleeding toes. I felt wonderful and weightless when I danced, as if I were flying. I'm not sure I could have articulated my feelings at the time, but I know now that dancing is a spiritual experience because it uplifts the soul.

My teachers recognized my developing talent and often asked me to perform at concerts and events around Hong Kong. My brother teasingly threatened to throw tomatoes at me when I was onstage, but that never happened. He knew better. Just because

I succeeded at ballet didn't mean I was a traditional girl. I was strong and spirited, maybe *too* spirited if you asked Aunty Nan. She and Daddy had four more children after Betty (who followed my lead and changed her name from Ka Ching to Betty Kwan after reading *Archie*)—Johnny, Annie, Reggie, and Teddy—but she considered me the most unmanageable of the seven.

I was about ten years old when I discovered a passion for flying kites and kite-catching on Homantin Hill, a game usually played by boys. I always knew when the weather was perfect for kite flying by the feel of the wind on my face and the sight of leaves dancing in the trees. When conditions were just right, I prepared like a warrior. My amah knew precisely what to do, dressing me in patched-up playclothes and pinning my two long pigtails close to my head to prevent anyone from pulling them.

The advantage of living on a hill was that I could see all around me. I perched on a rock and watched the kites flying above me like giant colorful birds. One memorable day, I spotted two kites "fighting." When two kites are close in the air, the objective is to slice the other flier's string, coated with glue and finely crushed glass resin, sending the vanquished kite to the ground. Then it's time to pounce! The person who's quick enough to catch the string keeps the kite.

Suddenly, one of the kites started to float in the breeze. The string was cut! I watched intently, calculating where the wind would carry it. The kite was heading in my direction! I ran toward it, spotted the string, and managed to grab it. Then I felt someone push me from behind, an interloper who snatched the string from my hand. The boy ran away with his prize, but I flew down the hill after him, knocking him to the ground and yanking back the kite string.

I screamed at him, telling him I got the kite first and reminded him of the Kite Catchers Code: The first one to get the string wins the kite. The boy gave me a dirty look, got up, and scurried away. Victory! The neighborhood boys may have been annoyed by my skills as a kite catcher, but they were also impressed. They called me the Flying Hen of Homantin Hill.

What did I learn that day? Reach for what you want, no matter how high you must leap, because you just might get it. And be prepared to fight for it because someone always wants to take it away.

These lessons served me well when I decided to attend boarding school in England. I had a plan, and it definitely involved a leap. First, I'd study at the Kingsmoor School in Glossop, Derbyshire. Then, I'd audition for the Royal Ballet School in London and become a ballerina. These were ambitious undertakings for an adolescent, but I believed a career in ballet was my destiny, and I was eager to get started.

My father may have been surprised when I approached him with the idea. Realistically, how could he object? When he was a boy, he went to the Bromsgrove School in Worcestershire, England, and he was sending my brother there. I proposed to follow in his footsteps. In my mind, it seemed perfectly natural that a twelve-year-old would travel six thousand miles to live among strangers in a strange land.

I won his permission, arrangements quickly fell into place as if they were meant to be, and I enrolled at Kingsmoor. I said goodbye to my family, not knowing what life would be like without them or when I would see them again. Then, I excitedly made my bold *grand jeté* to another continent and a new, independent life in England.

CHAPTER 3

When I arrived at Kingsmoor, I discovered that Glossop, a small town in Northern England, was a completely different world from the one I knew in Hong Kong. The rural landscape, with its hills, peaks, and endless moors, was something out of a Brontë novel, and the school itself, built in 1870 and covered with ivy, was an old English manor house. I settled into classes and joined the other students on long, rainy walks across the moors. The English, I learned, loved to walk, especially in bad weather.

I lived in a dormitory with other girls my age—some nice, some not. Occasionally, one of the meaner ones singled me out because I was Asian and said something nasty like "Chinese people eat dogs." I was a spitfire, still the Flying Hen of Homantin Hill, so slurs prompted me to fight back. We'd wrestle until the headmistress intervened and sternly ordered us to stop.

I didn't think of my classmate's insults as racist at the time. I was young and responded emotionally rather than intellectually. Children pick on each other for all sorts of reasons. I knew how to fight back and wasn't afraid to stand up for myself when a bully came my way.

Looking back, I'm surprised I wasn't homesick. My brother KK and I saw each other occasionally when he had time off from

Bromsgrove, but my father never visited. Instead, he sent me long, beautiful letters that transported me home to Kowloon. We wrote to each other faithfully, and I received a letter from home every two weeks—except for the one letter that went astray—it was in a mailbag on a BOAC plane that crashed. Miraculously, the missing letter was found in the rubble at the crash site and returned to my father, who sent it to me. When I held it in my hands, I liked to think it symbolized the unbreakable bond between us.

Daddy also sent me packages of my favorite foods, like salty plums and other Chinese delicacies. I think he was afraid I would starve to death in England. The girls in the dormitory looked at them askance and made faces. "What are you eating?" they asked suspiciously. "Grasshoppers?" I didn't mind their taunts because it meant I didn't have to share my treats.

I spent my first Christmas holiday with the headmaster and his family because traveling home to Hong Kong was too long an undertaking. Chinese New Year, my favorite holiday, came and went. Glossop had no fireworks, fragrant orchids, trays overflowing with candy, or bright red envelopes stuffed with money, and I missed the festivities. Fortunately, my second Christmas in England brought a happy and unexpected change of plan.

My mother's mother, Granny May, asked my father if he'd allow her grandchildren to spend the holidays at her home in Worthing, a seaside town in the south of England, near Brighton. Daddy agreed, and KK and I set out to see her.

Granny May had been in Hong Kong for my birth, but we'd lost contact since then, so I had no memories of her. Any feelings of estrangement disappeared moments after our emotional reunion. She was a wonderful, warm, lively, curious, and loving woman who, as my actual grandmother, became more like a mother to me than my own mother. Her home became my home, and we shared many happy times. She had so many interests, including touring castles in England. Whenever I had a holiday, she would take me with her and tell fascinating stories.

Granny May was nothing like Marquita. I discovered this firsthand at the age of fifteen when my mother again showed up unexpectedly during one of our holiday visits. She brought gifts for everyone as if that gesture could compensate for years of missed holidays, missed *everything*. Even though she was surrounded by family, she seemed out of place. She stayed overnight and left the next day, which was strange behavior for a mother who hadn't seen her children in such a long time. She was still a ghost in my life—just a whiff of perfume and a quick disappearance. That's what the word "mother" meant to me. I didn't brood about her neglect: That wasn't my nature. Instead, I concentrated on what made me happy.

Dancing made me happy. My father had promised I could go to the Royal Ballet School in London when I graduated from Kingsmoor, and I worked tirelessly toward that dream. I attended ballet classes in Manchester once a week, polishing my steps in preparation for the entrance exam, which I knew would be difficult. I was so excited when I got accepted! Life was going exactly as I'd planned it.

The youthquake that would upend music, raise skirt lengths, lower morals, and transform London into the swinging Mod capital of the world wasn't even a tremor when I moved there in 1956. My father considered the city safe and appropriate for his young daughter because it was probably not so different from the London *he* experienced as a student in the 1930s.

I lived in a boarding house and made friends with my class-mates. It was a short walk to school, where we spent most of our time, usually four hours a day, in dance classes. Studying ballet in this intense, demanding environment was more than mastering steps. My ballet training taught me determination, persistence, discipline, and the ability to hold myself accountable whenever I set out to accomplish a goal. These valuable lessons stayed with me long after I stepped away from the barre.

The Royal Ballet was my wonderland. Whenever an important dancer performed with the company, we were allowed to observe them at classes and rehearsals. I saw Margot Fonteyn, the Russian ballerina Galina Ulanova, and other legendary dancers who were magical and inspiring. And our lessons extended beyond the studio. Our teachers arranged visits to museums and galleries so we could cultivate a broader appreciation of the arts.

My father paid all my expenses, but my monthly allowance had to cover indulgences, and there always seemed to be more month than money. I was quite ambitious in those days and figured out ways to earn a little extra cash. I posed in my tutu for artists in life-study classes. And because my school had strong connections to the city's major cultural institutions, I auditioned for small parts in theatrical productions. In the Old Vic's 1957 staging of *A Midsummer Night's Dream*, I played a fairy (with billing in the program!) in the court of "First Fairy" Judi Dench. It was nice to earn pocket money, but I really appreciated the opportunity to watch legendary actors at work and develop my stage skills. I saw Laurence Olivier perform Othello and listened in awe as the audience recited with him.

I felt instantly at home in London because KK was nearby, beginning his studies at the London School of Architecture. He was a considerate older brother who always found a reason to drop in on me, sometimes surprising me with my favorite treat of strawberries and cream. He introduced me to his wide circle of friends, who quickly became my friends. Many were from Hong Kong, so we had a lot in common. They all had motorbikes, so we explored the city together, speeding through London's winding streets. One friend who had a car tried to teach me how to drive, but after a few attempts, we agreed I would be better off learning at a proper driving school.

We were always hungry but could afford only the cheapest restaurants, which usually turned out to be Chinese or Indian. Unlike many young ballerinas, I could eat the foods I loved without worrying about my weight. I was slim, and my size never changed.

Boys? Oh yes! Considering that we had no adult supervision and could have gone wild, our "romantic" relationships were very innocent. I had schoolgirl crushes and went on dates with the young men in my group, but I never got serious about anyone because I was serious about my dancing.

In 1959, I went home to Hong Kong for the summer. I was looking ahead to the future and thinking about opening a ballet school. I certainly had the qualifications after my years of studying. While considering my options, I relaxed at home, enjoying the company of my family and friends and indulging in all the wonderful foods that weren't available in London.

Everyone was talking about the bestselling book, *The World of Suzie Wong*, set in Wan Chai, Hong Kong's old waterfront district. Richard Mason's novel tells the story of Suzie Wong, a spirited and highly principled young prostitute who views her questionable profession as her only means of survival in post–World War II Hong Kong, a world where the rules have been rewritten by economic and societal forces beyond her control.

She meets Robert Lomax, a British artist living in Hong Kong, who learns that Suzie is so much more than she appears to be. The mother of a young child, Suzie works as a prostitute to support her son. Lomax is charmed by her unusual combination of worldliness and innocence. She knows how to survive in her harsh reality, but she also dreams of a different world, one with love, happiness, and fairy-tale endings. Their developing relationship is threatened by racial prejudice and class and cultural differences, but they learn to trust each other and overcome the forces working against them.

My world in Hong Kong couldn't be further from the one experienced by the heroine in the novel, a working girl in a backstreet bar, but I appreciated that this beautiful love story challenged readers to look beyond the Asian stereotypes propagated by the war to see the humanity of Suzie, a girl who wanted a better life.

When the film was announced, there was widespread speculation about who would be cast in the title role, the assumption being that the part would go to a Hollywood actress—they always did. In the 1955 blockbuster *Love Is a Many-Splendored Thing*, Jennifer Jones played Dr. Han Suyin, a widowed physician from Mainland China who had a doomed interracial romance with an American reporter played by William Holden. The filmmakers relied on Ben Nye, a master of movie makeup, to apply prosthetics to her eyes to give them the stereotypical Asian slant. I loved the movie, and honestly, it didn't occur to me when I watched it that Dr. Suyin (who also wrote the autobiographical book on which the film is based) should have been played by an Asian. I was blind to even the *possibility* because in those days, it just wasn't done.

William Holden was set to play Robert Lomax, now reimagined as an American artist who falls in love with Suzie Wong. Audiences loved "Golden Holden," as the trade papers dubbed him, for his performances in *Sunset Boulevard, Stalag 17, Sabrina,* and *The Bridge on the River Kwai* (and later in his career, *Network*, Paddy Chayefsky's bold satire of the media). Holden was nominated for three Oscars and named "Most Popular Male Star" by *Photoplay* in 1955 and 1956. His talent was so great that he could play an action hero or a romantic lead. And even when he lost Audrey Hepburn to Humphrey Bogart in *Sabrina*, he won her heart in real life. She was his great love, but the one who got away, a breakup that seemed to be one of the causes of his ongoing battle with depression.

Surprisingly, Ray Stark, the film's producer, announced his intention to break tradition and find a young *Asian* actress to play the female lead. It was an extraordinary idea at the time, but Ray Stark was no ordinary producer. As a powerful talent agent, he'd represented Richard Burton, Lana Turner, William Holden, Kirk Douglas, and other superstars. *The World of Suzie Wong* was his first foray into producing at Seven Arts, his newly launched company. His *first*, but far from his last. Ray Stark would produce many blockbusters and classics, including *Funny Girl, The Owl and the Pussycat, The Way We Were, The Goodbye Girl, Smokey and the Bandit, Annie,* and *Steel Magnolias*.

He oversaw every detail of his maiden film, every press release, every dollar of the budget, and every casting decision, including the hunt for the perfect Suzie. He embarked on a much-publicized, worldwide search, with stops in Honolulu, Tokyo, and Manila, and arrived in Hong Kong on August 15, 1959. A notice in the newspaper invited "girls aged 18–22" who were "innocent but vivacious" and "who must have an interesting and magnetic attraction" to come to the Cathay studio for an open casting call.

I saw the story in the newspaper and suspected my favorite young Chinese actresses would show up at the audition, so I thought it would be fun to see them in person. Getting in that day would be easy because my father designed the studio for its owner, my great-uncle Loke Wan Tho, who was my great-grandfather Loke Yew's son.

He was a fascinating man. In his twenties, he fled from Malaysia to escape the Japanese. His ship was attacked, and he was gravely injured, suffering severe burns and temporary blindness. Like a phoenix, Loke Wan Tho rose from the ashes to build the massive Cathay Organization, which included two movie studios, theaters, production facilities, hotels, and restaurants throughout Asia. He created such a vast empire—and became so rich— that he was called the Paul Getty of the Far East. He was also a renowned ornithologist and photographer. His life came to a tragic end in 1964 when he, his wife, and the studio executives traveling with them died in a plane crash flying home from a film festival.

On the day of the auditions, I went to the studio and settled into a corner where I wouldn't be in the way. I knew what it was like to work onstage, but I hadn't had any film experience, so I was curious to watch the process, which involved many bright lights and a crowd of people waiting. Some would-be "Suzies" were nervous and wooden; others flirted confidently with the camera, hoping to demonstrate their "innocent and vivacious" charm.

At a certain point, I realized one of the scouts was watching me. Then, he headed in my direction. As he approached, I deliberated: If he asked me to leave, should I tell him Luke Wan Tho was my great-uncle? Or should I go quietly?

Before I could decide, he asked if I was there to test for the role. I explained that I was a dancer, not an actress, and I was visiting the set. He overruled my protests and persuaded me to step in front of the camera to do a screen test. *This is an experience*, I thought. I was sure whatever I did in those few minutes wasn't good. I hadn't prepared, so I was completely natural, and a young girl being a young girl wasn't likely to impress anyone. That was fine. I wasn't trying to be Suzie Wong.

I left the studio and went back to my real life.

Time passed, then Daddy received the unexpected letter from Ray Stark, who must have understood that the proper way to approach a girl from a good family in Hong Kong was through her father. He had seen my test and thought I had so much potential that he offered me a six-month contract with Seven Arts, at a salary of $300 a week, and the opportunity to study acting in Hollywood—all because he believed *I* might be his Suzie Wong. If my father approved, arrangements could be made immediately.

I was thrilled and ready to start packing, mainly because I had always wanted to visit Los Angeles. An extended trip, with a salary and the possibility of a starring role in an important movie, seemed like an offer I'd be crazy to refuse. Before the conversation could go any further, Seven Arts had to convince my father that I would have a suitable place to live. We didn't know anyone in Hollywood, and he insisted his daughter was not going there alone without some measure of security.

Seven Arts proposed the Hollywood Studio Club, explaining that it was a residence for women who aspired to have careers in the movie business. The club, which sounded very much like a sorority, provided housing, meals, and social activities *and* enforced strict codes of conduct, which meant NO men were allowed anywhere except the approved spaces on the first floor. The Mediterranean-style building, reminiscent of a cloister, was even designed by a woman, Julia Morgan, the architect who worked on Hearst Castle for twenty-eight years. This haven of morality in the heart of Hollywood seemed above reproach, so my father gave his permission. I was on my way.

CHAPTER 4

The fourteen-hour flight from Hong Kong to Los Angeles on a Pan American clipper was an adventure. Meals—three courses, with a selection of delicious desserts—were served on a tray covered with a white tablecloth set with real cutlery. We stopped in Honolulu to go through customs, and as soon as I got off the airplane, I felt the warm tropical breeze and inhaled the heady scent of blossoms. The Hawaiians who greeted us had garlands of flowers around their necks, and some women wore flowers in their hair. The place had such a beautiful aura that I promised myself I'd return.

I landed in Los Angeles, famous for its picture-postcard palm trees and bright blue skies. It was autumn, and in the coming weeks, I marveled that it never ever rained. I'm told the city often had a curtain of smog at the time, but I remember endless sunshine.

The Hollywood Studio Club, while not precisely the chaste sorority my father imagined, was a wonderful place where a clue-less young newcomer to the city could make friends, have fun, and feel safe. The club, described by one newspaper as the place "Where Hollywood's Good Girls Go," had been home to many rising stars, including Kim Novak, Rita Moreno, and Marilyn

Monroe, who, ironically, posed for her famous nude photos while living there to earn the fifty dollars she needed to pay her rent.

When I went down to breakfast my first morning, I looked around the room and realized I had never seen so many beautiful women in one place, and they were from all over the world: France, Spain, Italy, and other places. Miss Williams, who managed the club, kept a watchful eye on us while we were on the premises. Dances, and any other social activities involving the opposite sex, were chaperoned, which was funny considering that many of the club's aspiring actresses cultivated the blonde, big-bosomed sexpot look perennially popular in Hollywood. I doubt they ever thought about being on their best behavior.

I didn't fit that mold. My dark hair was long and straight, not blonde and coiffed, and my clothes were simple and classic. When I dressed up, I usually wore a cheongsam from Hong Kong instead of a low-cut cocktail dress and furs. My unusual look didn't prevent a young man from approaching me the night I attended my first social gathering at the club. I was a little nervous, so I sat shyly on the sidelines. When he asked me to dance, I shook my head and said, "No, I can't dance."

Where did that come from? I was a trained dancer! Subsequently, that young man became one of my dear friends, and we still laugh about the story today.

The men who flocked to the Studio Club like bees to honey were as stunning as the women. Every night, the parking lot was filled with flashy sports cars and their handsome—and sometimes famous—owners. Cary Grant, Frank Sinatra, and other boldface names straight out of *Photoplay* (one night I remember meeting a very handsome Roger Moore in the garden) visited the young ladies, who made a dramatic entrance by sweeping down the staircase leading to the club's reception area. What happened *after* they left the building was none of Miss William's business.

I rented a snappy Austin Healy convertible—bright turquoise with a black top—and drove everywhere. One day, I decided to go to the beach but didn't know where it was, so I asked someone for directions. "Just take Sunset all the way," they told me, adding that it would take a long time. I figured I had all the time in the world, so I started driving. I discovered you could drive, drive, and drive and still not get anywhere in Los Angeles. I'd never seen a street so long as Sunset Boulevard! When I finally got to the beach, it was time to turn around and go home. *That* was my big adventure.

Most of the time, I concentrated on my acting classes. Seven Arts had set me up with Salka Viertel, mother of novelist and screenwriter Peter Viertel and a close friend and mentor to Greta Garbo. Her workshops were fascinating, and I met my friend Susan Kohner, an up-and-coming actress who had recently starred in the blockbuster *Imitation of Life* with Lana Turner, John Gavin, and Sandra Dee. Susan's character, the light-skinned daughter of a Black housekeeper, derails her life when she runs away from home and pretends to be white. Susan was excellent in the role. She stole the film from Lana Turner—no easy feat for a young actress—and was nominated for an Academy Award and won a Golden Globe for Best Supporting Actress. Casting her, the daughter of Mexican actress Lupita Tovar and Austrian émigré Paul Kohner, as a fair-skinned African American was Hollywood being Hollywood.

My best lessons were with Jeff Corey, an actor who became a teacher after the House Un-American Activities Committee blacklisted him for refusing to divulge the names of alleged communists in Hollywood. He began by offering acting classes in his garage and quickly became one of Hollywood's most prominent coaches, known for his ability to mentor young talents, including James Dean, Jane Fonda, and Jack Nicholson.

I worked with Jeff to prepare for my screen test for *The World of Suzie Wong*. During our improvisational exercises, I learned to trust my intuition and draw on my personality and experiences to create a character. As I discovered when studying ballet, I had to use my body as an instrument.

Suzie was a complicated role for a first-time actress because I had to convince the audience to suspend their 1950s preconceptions about prostitutes and accept her as a sympathetic heroine. To do this, I had to understand her and find our connections— the basic human behavior we shared—so I could transcend the differences in our circumstances. Suzie was curious, optimistic, loyal, generous, and loving. Her profession was the least interesting thing about her.

I read books about prostitutes and discussed their motivations with Jeff to internalize the character. Nothing shocked me because I learned that many prostitutes turned to the profession out of desperation. Like Suzie, they did what they had to do.

One of the most valuable lessons I learned in my sessions with Jeff is that an actress must reach inside herself, use the emotions and behavior that can help bring a character to life, and discard the ones that get in the way. I could play a prostitute, a murderer, or the girl next door if I understood her psychology because then I could make her real. And however difficult or daring the role might be, I should be willing to try.

It was an exciting time to be an actress. Although I was new to Hollywood, I could see that the movie business was changing.

The big movies, the ones advertised on the giant billboards lining Sunset Boulevard, were studio productions. *Ben Hur, Imitation of Life, Some Like It Hot.* But the "kids" in my acting classes were excited about Truffaut's *The 400 Blows* and the French New Wave, the gritty, "kitchen sink" dramas coming from England, and the homegrown "B" movies Roger Corman produced with astonishing speed (and very little money). Corman took risks and was willing to give fledgling actors their first leading roles—Charles Bronson in *Machine Gun Kelly* and Jack Nicholson in *The Cry Baby Killer.* Even when the movies were terrible, they suggested a younger, more controversial, and enthusiastically anti-studio approach to filmmaking was challenging the old guard.

Jean Negulesco, *Suzie Wong's* director, asked me to come to his house at 10 p.m. one night to "rehearse" some scenes. Negulesco had made several high-grossing films, like *How to Marry a Millionaire, The Best of Everything,* and *Three Coins in the Fountain* and was the epitome of old Hollywood in all the worst ways. I might have been naïve, but I was never stupid. Even I knew that "rehearse" was code for a session on the notorious casting couch. I immediately called Ray and told him about Negulesco's invitation. "Don't you think it's rather late to go to his house to rehearse?" I asked. I'm not sure what Ray said to him, but I never heard from Negulesco again.

Finally, with Ray Stark's encouragement, I filmed two screen tests while the producers dragged their heels about their casting decision. The suspense was terrible.

I worked hard to develop my acting skills, but the news was not good. Ray called to tell me that Paramount, the studio underwriting the film, decided to cast France Nuyen, a French actress who broke out as Liat in *South Pacific,* and was currently playing Suzie Wong in the Broadway stage play adapted from the novel, which also starred a young William Shatner. She was the right age and type for *Suzie Wong* and had more experience.

But Nuyen was best known for her tumultuous love affair with Marlon Brando, a relationship dissected by every gossip columnist and chronicled in every tabloid. Would he marry her? Had they broken up? The speculation was fierce and kept her name in the Hollywood headlines.

I should have known she would get the part. Any studio would see her as the safer—and more exploitable—bet. But I was very disappointed, even heartbroken. Sensing my disappointment, Ray made a suggestion. Seven Arts was one of the producing partners of the Broadway play. He wanted me to join the New York theater production to understudy Jeri Miyazaki, the actress taking over for Nuyen when she left to film *Suzie Wong*; then, I could continue as a bar girl and lead understudy on the company's national tour.

Now that was an exciting idea! Live in New York City, work on Broadway, and then tour for six months? I would have the chance to see the country and determine if I really wanted to be an actress. If this was a consolation prize, it was a very good one, and I agreed to do it.

I said goodbye to my new friends at the Studio Club and wondered what would happen to them. They came to Hollywood with burning ambition and high hopes, but most would not realize their dreams of becoming Marilyn Monroe. It was hardest for the actresses. Eventually, the auditions dried up, or the girls got tired of constant rejection, and they went home to very different lives, maybe *good* lives with husbands and children, but not the lives they imagined.

In New York, I moved into the Barbizon Hotel on East 63rd Street, another storied refuge for women and essentially the East Coast version of the Studio Club. A home for actresses, models, writers, students at the Katharine Gibbs secretarial school, and other working women (including Grace Kelly, Sylvia Plath, Joan Didion, Ali McGraw, and Liza Minnelli), the Barbizon enforced strict rules to keep the "wolves of New York," otherwise known as *men,* a safe distance from their female guests. Gentlemen were allowed only on the first floor. Most women, however young, wore hats, gloves, and stockings, a fashionable form of armor signaling they were *ladies.*

I didn't spend much time at the hotel because I was rehearsing day and night at the theater. But I knew Daddy would approve of the Barbizon's air of gentility *and* the presence of Mae Sibley, the associate manager, who was a vigilant watchdog.

We had very little time to whip the national company into shape, so I was grateful for all my ballet training because I had the stamina to get through it. I was comfortable onstage as a "Flower of the Bar" and an understudy to Suzie, and I was excited about the performances ahead. I stopped thinking about the film, which had started shooting in Hong Kong under the direction of Negulesco—that ship had sailed—and I concentrated on my new career.

I made lifelong friends during rehearsals, especially my cast-mates Flavia Hsu Kingman and Parke Perine, who later married and gave me the honor of being godmother to their daughters Laura and Andrea. We'd be traveling by train during the tour, and my experienced friends told me the most important thing was to buy a trunk. I didn't even know what a trunk was, but they explained it was a giant suitcase that had to be large enough to fit everything I owned while we went from New York to Los Angeles, with many stops in between.

My father dispatched KK to New York to check up on me, and I loved having him as a companion. He stayed for two weeks, attending rehearsals and exploring the city with me when I had a free moment.

Then, the tour began. Everything moved so fast! We'd set up in a theater, play for a few nights, pack up, and have another opening night in a new city.

We had just arrived in Toronto when the stage manager told me Ray Stark was on the telephone. He barely said hello before he asked me a question I never expected to hear.

"Can you come to London immediately to test with William Holden? Nuyen and Negulesco are off the film."

"Are you *crazy*?" I said—momentarily forgetting that I was a twenty-year-old understudy while he was one of the most successful powerbrokers in Hollywood. Was he really asking me to drop everything and come to London because he needed a new Suzie Wong? I had so many questions. What happened to France Nuyen? Why was the production shutting down? They had been shooting in Hong Kong for two months, so something must have gone very wrong for Ray to abandon all that expensive footage and start over.

"I'll tell you everything in London," Ray said hurriedly as he offered a few details. Nuyen was out, he repeated, but he didn't explain why. Subsequently, a press announcement cited her "collapse on set" and "nervous exhaustion" as the reasons. But there were rumors that her turbulent relationship with Brando, which seemed to have ended dramatically, caused her to overeat and lose the girlish figure she needed to play Suzie.

Negulesco was out, too (I wasn't sorry to hear that after his inappropriate—and inept—attempt to seduce me). He was replaced by Richard Quine, whose most recent credit was *Bell, Book, and Candle*, starring Kim Novak and Jimmy Stewart.

The World of Suzie Wong was a mess and needed a fresh start . . . *yesterday*.

I wanted to race to London but couldn't imagine walking out on my responsibilities. What about David Merrick, the play's producer, who was scary on a good day?

Producers are quick to come up with answers, and Ray Stark was no exception. He said I should tell the production I had an emergency, that my father was gravely ill, and I had to go home. That excuse didn't sit well with me, but Ray was one of the show's producers and assured me he would take care of everything. I still thought he was crazy to offer this opportunity to an absolute nobody, but I flew out on the next plane.

When I landed, I experienced a different London from the one I had left six months ago. Was it only six months? Gone were the days of boys and motorbikes. A chauffeur met me at the airport and whisked me to the studio, where wardrobe, hair, and makeup rushed to get me in character for my screen test. Before I could say "Suzie Wong," I was *her*, dressed in a cheongsam, my long hair trailing down my back.

I should have been terrified to test with one of the biggest stars in Hollywood, but I saw right away that Willian Holden was a kind and generous actor committed to my success. He was warm and personable and invited me to call him "Bill."

I wasn't walking in cold because I had tested before and spent weeks learning my lines for the show. "For goodness' sake," I said as we ran through our scene. I sounded convincing because

I used that expression in real life. I felt good about the test. And, in the back of my mind, I remembered an experience I had when I was sixteen when my cousin Robert took me to see a fortune teller in Hong Kong. The seer looked at me and predicted I would become an actress. I protested and told him I was a ballet dancer and had no interest in acting, but the fortune teller had a different vision of the future and insisted on having the last word. "You will be a famous actress," he called out as we left.

I hoped he was right, but the decision rested with Ray, Bill, and Richard Quine.

They approved! I was twenty years old and going to be the star of a major motion picture. I had no time to celebrate because my director was waiting for me on set—possibly the same set in London where my father met my mother, so I stepped in front of the camera.

CHAPTER 5

The real Bill Holden was even more interesting than the movie star. He was what we used to call a "man's man" who wore his accolades, awards, and stardom lightly. None of that mattered to Bill: he made his living as an actor but was passionate about his other interests and had many.

Bill loved being in Asia—at one point, he maintained an apartment in Hong Kong—and was fascinated by Asian art. He forged relationships with the best art dealers and became quite a collector. He also invested in Hong Kong businesses and was part owner of the local radio station. As for the speculation that Bill was an operative for the CIA—I wouldn't be surprised. He spent time at Hong Kong's Foreign Correspondent Club, where journalists exchanged information, especially concerning enigmatic China, which was off-limits at the time. It would have been just like Bill to see it as his duty to report any information he overheard to the US government.

Bill had been a movie star since the late 1930s, and as he got older, he developed a drinking problem. He may have had private demons, but I never saw Bill intoxicated when we were filming—he hit his mark, remembered his lines, and was professional in every way. There was no Method in Bill's performance—none of the tics, self-examination, or self-obsession that became a trademark of the younger generation of actors: He inhabited his role, intuitively making the right choices for his character in his less-is-more way. It was exciting to see how much he could accomplish with the flick of an eyebrow or a subtle gesture. He did everything with such ease.

I watched Bill and our accomplished co-stars Sylvia Syms and Michael Wilding, learning that working with talented professionals elevates your own work. While filming a love scene one day, Bill noticed an unflattering shadow that obscured my face and gently repositioned me until the light was just right. He wanted me to look good and was always generous with his expertise, encouragement, and flattery. "When Nancy is in a scene, I have to come back twice to find myself," he said teasingly. "That's the story of my life—my co-star takes the acting honors, and I take the money."

When a reporter suggested Bill was coaching me, he refused to take any credit for my performance. "No one can show another how to act," he said. "I've given Nancy pointers, true. But to act, you've got to have the feeling and instinct within. Nancy has both." And if someone tried to suggest I was just another pretty face, he'd shut them down with a few well-chosen words. "Nancy is the first actress I've worked with who's a philosopher," he said. "She's wonderful. Period."

He was wonderful, and I'm forever grateful to him for being a mentor and for helping me to believe in myself.

My Cinderella experience included staying at the Connaught, one of London's best hotels, and having a driver to take me wherever I wanted to go. On top of that, I was making money. The one thing I didn't have was free time. I rarely went out with my friends from school because I was always filming or preparing for the next day's shoot. Eventually, I figured out how to have the fun come to me. One day, Ray approached me on the set and asked why my room service bill was so high. He couldn't believe that I could eat so much! I confessed that I invited my brother KK and his friends to have dinner with me on weekends. They were students who lived on their pocket money, so sometimes I treated them to a good meal courtesy of room service. Ray had a big heart and approved the expense.

When I did go out, it was usually with people from the film. I had a lovely dinner with Bill, his wife, Ardis, and their sons Scott and Peter. On set, I played ping-pong with the boys. I was still a kid at heart.

Thanks to Bill, I met David Lean, my favorite director. They'd worked together on *The Bridge on the River Kwai* and had a spirited reunion at lunch. I sat there in awe, listening to every word of these two very talented and successful men.

I loved every day of making *Suzie Wong*, except one when a disagreement exploded over my costume and prompted me to rebel. The scene called for Bill's character, Robert Lomax, to angrily rip off my dress because he objected to Suzie's fussy Western attire, which she wore to prove her so-called sophistication. Wardrobe had selected sexy black undergarments for the big reveal, but I was modest and secretly substituted a full slip, which was *not* what Dick Quine expected to see.

All hell broke loose.

Today, an intimacy coordinator would be on set to ensure I was comfortable with such a sensitive scene, but we didn't have that kind of protection in 1960. I was expected to follow the director's instructions. When I refused, crying because I was embarrassed to wear something so revealing, I was reminded that it was part of the job. Were they taking advantage of my youth and inexperience? Absolutely, but I didn't have a choice. Ray improved the situation by promising to close the set to all but necessary crew when we filmed.

I dried my eyes, dressed in the approved lingerie, and went back to work, telling myself I was being professional. We got through the scene, but I felt vulnerable. I had seen a darker side of the glittering world of moviemaking and promised myself I'd navigate it carefully in the future.

I experienced another clash of wills when I was invited to attend a Command Performance of *The Last Angry Man*, hosted by Prince Philip, the Duke of Edinburgh. Unfortunately, we had just filmed a fight between me and a bar girl. Richard Quine wanted the scene to look realistic and encouraged us to make it a real fight. It was so real that I ended up with a black eye and couldn't work for a few days. I wanted to attend the event but was so unhappy about my appearance. *Suzie Wong's* publicist suggested I cover my injury with a black eye patch. I could see that he was excited about the idea because he thought it would attract attention from the press, which was the last thing *I* wanted. Furthermore, I was still a British subject and did not intend to look like a pirate when I met royalty. I solved the problem with makeup and had a lovely evening.

We spent three months filming in London, then headed to Hong Kong to shoot exteriors. In both locations, Ray depended on me to be his liaison with the Asian actors and extras who had never worked on an American production. I explained each scene and told them what they were expected to do. Ray said I was so helpful that I was practically an assistant director. The experience made me want to learn more about what goes on behind the camera, and I paid close attention to the director, cinematographer, and technicians to better understand the process.

When we arrived in Hong Kong harbor, I had no idea the city was caught up in *Suzie Wong* fever until I stepped off the boat and was mobbed by photographers and excited fans. It sounds strange to call them fans because the film wasn't finished, and no one had seen my work. I think they came to give their hometown girl an enthusiastic welcome.

The reporters bombarded me with questions. Where would I go, and what would I do in Hong Kong? I told them I'd work, spend time with my family, and eat vast quantities of chow fun and mangoes. "Nothing in the world can beat the food in Hong Kong," I boasted.

I didn't tell them that I'd arranged to meet with some prostitutes for research while I was in Hong Kong. The preparation I'd done with Jeff Corey could take me only so far. I wanted a firsthand connection with a real-life Suzie Wong to understand my character better.

Character is an important word here. Then, and for years to come, I was asked why I accepted the role. Later in my career, I produced a tai chi instructional tape in the 1980s and appeared on a San Francisco television show to promote it. The interviewer, who was Chinese, abruptly changed the subject from tai chi to *Suzie Wong* and said to me, "You did *The World of Suzie Wong*, and you played that prostitute. And because you played that prostitute, everybody thinks that all Chinese women are prostitutes."

I felt blindsided—and offended—by her sudden attack but reacted coolly. "I beg your pardon," I said.

"Well, because of you, they think Chinese women are whores!" she persisted.

I couldn't believe that she said that to me. Ridiculous as it was, the misconception was worth addressing.

"I am not a prostitute. I'm an actor," I snapped. "Actors play roles—that's our job."

To elaborate, we reach into our imaginations and create characters who may have nothing to do with our real lives. We tell stories that we hope will inspire the audience to believe—and understand—the people we portray, whether it's a housewife, a serial killer, or a prostitute. If it's a good role, I'll play it.

When I was making *The World of Suzie Wong*, I was committed to creating an authentic character instead of a stereotype. The prostitutes in Hong Kong told me they came to the job out of desperation. Many were refugees who'd fled China with no way to support themselves and, in some cases, their children. They worked as prostitutes because they had no other options. They deserved compassion, not condemnation.

Several years later, I learned more about the subject when I was casting a film that included an innocent nude scene. None of the actresses we approached would agree to do it, so I had the idea of bringing in a prostitute to audition, figuring nudity was part of the job in that particular profession. But the woman we interviewed refused and seemed slightly taken aback by my request. "If I'm naked in a film, everybody sees it," she balked. "When I do it, it's *private*." Every profession, even prostitution, has its code.

I'm not sure the insensitive interviewer understood what I was saying about acting or prostitution, but it was important to me to educate her. The movie wasn't a documentary. Ray Stark set out to make a love story about a man and a woman—the differences that ripped them apart and the love that brought them together. I think Ray was unhappy with Negulesco's footage because there was too much gritty realism and not enough romance, which is why he replaced him as the director.

While we were shooting in Hong Kong, I felt the same sense of displacement I'd experienced in London. Everything was familiar but somehow different. I stayed at the Peninsula Hotel with the cast, so I'd be closer to the locations, and I visited my family in Kowloon when I had free time. At my father's house, I was still "Big Daughter," the eldest girl in the family. But at work, I was at the center of a multimillion-dollar movie and a media frenzy fueled by the Paramount publicity department. The attention was exhilarating *and* exhausting. One day, I was out window-shopping when I noticed a crowd gathering behind me. I turned to see what they were looking at, and it was me!

We shot a scene on the Kowloon ferry, and I instantly recalled a funny memory of my father. Ferry tickets were purchased according to class. First-class passengers sat at the boat's top while third-class ticket holders were restricted to the bottom. The price difference was negligible, but my father refused to travel in "First" because the passengers below had a shorter distance to cover when they disembarked. "It's less walking," he always said. Daddy was eccentric that way.

I turned twenty-one while in Hong Kong and enjoyed quite a celebration. When we were shooting the ferry scene, I was presented with an enormous cake shaped like a Chinese pagoda, set atop a cage holding twenty-one homing pigeons. When I blew out the candles, the birds were supposed to take flight, but they refused to exit their cage until someone gave them a gentle poke.

Shooting wrapped a few days later. I did it! I felt such a sense of accomplishment. Then, I learned that *making* a film is only one part of the process. The release of *The World of Suzie Wong*, especially the massive publicity campaign, would require me to visit three continents, walk endless red carpets, and travel accompanied by a chaperone.

My Hollywood adventure was about to begin.

CHAPTER 6

Ray Stark and his wife, Fran, kicked off the *Suzie Wong* publicity marathon by hosting a party to introduce me to Hollywood. Fran said she first had the idea while the film was shooting in Hong Kong. She saw some Chinese lanterns in a store and told Ray, "Let's buy them and have a party." When the Starks threw a party, which they frequently did, their guest list was so impressive that gossip columnists joked it was far easier to mention the handful of stars who *didn't* attend than it was to name the hundreds who did. My party was no exception.

Fran, the daughter of legendary entertainer Fanny Brice (the singer and comedienne Barbra Streisand brought to life in the movie *Funny Girl*), was an exceptional hostess who learned all about the good life from her famous mother. She grew up under the watchful eye of a French governess, summered in Europe, developed her own highly evolved sense of style, wore couture clothes and statement jewelry, and frequently was named on the best-dressed list. She was Hollywood royalty while Ray, an agent-turned-producer, was an A-list powerbroker. Together, they were Hollywood aristocracy.

The Starks had recently moved to their new residence in Holmby Hills, the former home of Humphrey Bogart and Lauren Bacall. Their collection of Impressionist and Contemporary paintings hung inside the house, and in years to come, Ray added an impressive sculpture garden with works by Henry Moore, Alexander Calder, and Aristide Maillol. He protected his prize artwork with a whimsical decoy—a prop police car given to him by television producer Aaron Spelling—permanently parked in the driveway to deter would-be thieves.

The night of the party, the Stark estate was transformed into a lush oriental garden illuminated by the lanterns that traveled all the way from Hong Kong. The grounds were covered with an enormous circus tent spacious enough to seat three hundred guests at a formal, multicourse dinner. The staff rivaled the crew on a Ray Stark production, including *three* orchestras instead of Fran's customary two, forty waiters, a wine steward, twelve bartenders, fourteen parking valets, six coat-check stations, and an army of behind-the-scenes caterers and kitchen workers—"So nobody went danceless, hungry, thirsty, coatless, or home in the wrong car," one columnist quipped.

Fran's unerring eye for detail extended to me. She asked Guy LaRoche, her favorite couturier, to make me a red beaded sheath dress reminiscent of a cheongsam with an eye-catching slit on the side. The studio arranged for my date—Prince Charming was supposed to be heartthrob Tab Hunter, who couldn't make it because he was filming *The Pleasure of His Company*, but handsome Tom Tryon, fresh from Paramount's breakout hit *I Married a Monster from Outer Space*, stepped in to be my escort at the last minute.

Young Hollywood was represented by several headliner couples that night, notably Warren Beatty and his girlfriend Joan Collins, and Kim Novak and *Suzie Wong* director Richard Quine. But I was more interested in *old* Hollywood. The stars I watched while growing up seemed to have stepped off the screen and were all around me, still larger than life. Merle Oberon, Edward G. Robinson, George Burns, Milton Berle, Joan Crawford, flaunting flaming red hair (she, Roz Russell, and Norma Shearer had to be seated at separate tables because they couldn't be within clawing distance of each other), and many more famous faces. Kirk Douglas, whose wife, Anne, had injured herself in a fall, picked her up in his arms and carried her across the room to a chair, his grand romantic gesture winning a round of applause from delighted onlookers.

Charming David Niven, the suave actor I admired in *Around the World in Eighty Days* and *Bonjour Tristesse*, came over to introduce himself. He looked at me, then at the glittering crowd, and offered a few words of advice to the Hollywood newcomer who was probably looking (and feeling) a little overwhelmed. "Keep your feet on the ground, and don't let all this go to your head," he said.

In the spirit of the party's "East meets West" theme, we dined on a Hollywood caterer's idea of Cantonese classics, including fried shrimp, eggrolls, and hollowed pineapple halves filled with ice cream, leading a funny, if politically incorrect, Groucho Marx to joke, "Cantonese food? We'll all be hungry in thirty minutes."

My oft-repeated assessment of the evening in newspapers across the country was "Nice, but I don't like large parties." I didn't mean to sound rude or ungrateful; the Starks had gone through a lot of trouble to make my Hollywood coming-out party memorable. But when I'm asked a question, I answer it honestly, a trait that often startled the journalists I met over the next few months.

In the time leading up to the film's release, the Paramount publicity machine devised a massive *Suzie Wong* campaign and decided I would be its hook, figuring that the best way to sell Suzie was to offer a real-life China Doll—*me*. I was sent out on a multicity publicity tour with a "chaperone," an older woman who functioned as a press secretary. She handled my schedule and coordinated my interviews. But she was also there to ensure my safety when we traveled cross-country. I think the studio was afraid that when we were in conservative places in the South, someone might say something derogatory or insulting because I am Asian.

They were right to be concerned. When I was in the stage company of *The World of Suzie Wong*, some hotels in the South refused to give the Asian actors rooms, so the manager had to arrange for separate accommodations. I left the tour before we went to those places, but my friends told me about them.

Actually, everyone was polite and respectful when I did publicity, and I didn't encounter any racism in person...

Most interviews began and ended the same way. The journalist walked in wanting to see Suzie Wong—the sultry yum-yum girl (who couldn't be further away from my reality) and viewed me through that lens because it was a better story. I became "Hollywood's Honey from Hong Kong," as if, like Suzie, I had been plucked from a bar in far-off Hong Kong and transported to the new world to be a celebrity.

The fan magazines were the worst because they were in the business of fabricating stories to seduce their readers into coming back for more. They often put a tabloid spin on studio press releases, and most of what appeared on their pages was fiction.

The journalists who wrote for reputable outlets should have had a higher standard. Yet they insisted on attributing quotes to me that perpetuated xenophobic tropes of a Chinese person speaking English and bore no resemblance to the way I sounded. One reporter asked about my measurements (rude!) and wrote that I answered, "Just say I big for China, enough for England, maybe small for Italy." A funny line, but it wasn't *mine*.

Another asked if I exaggerated the wiggle in my walk and wrote that I answered, "No! Can't help my walk. Must go the way my body takes me." Where were my pronouns? Why did I sound like I learned English last week when I had spoken it my entire life? My father studied at Cambridge, and I was educated at a convent in Hong Kong, a private school in England, and the Royal Ballet in London. I spoke "the King's English" and probably employed better diction and grammar than most Americans. But I was made to sound like I had just gotten off some boat.

And the writer who described me as "an impish Chinese doll with a slant-eyed walk…that makes Marilyn Monroe look like she's in low gear" should have been ashamed of his maladroit metaphor. Legs don't have eyes, slanted or otherwise.

On the other hand, I never minded being compared to Audrey Hepburn or Brigitte Bardot!

By late October, I was already tired of the subject because I *hated* talking about myself. When a reporter asked how I got discovered, I sighed, "Here we go again." When another asked if my eyelashes were real, I moved closer to him and said, "Here. Pull," proving they *were* real. I think my publicists feared what I might say—or do—next. Young stars were supposed to be eager to please and malleable, but I was outspoken and said exactly what was on my mind.

A cover shoot for *Life* magazine was an important entry on my schedule and a real coup for Paramount. This prime real estate would promote *The World of Suzie Wong* to the popular magazine's seven million readers. Photographer Bert Stern, known for his captivating shots of Marilyn Monroe, began our session in the studio, where I posed in a yellow cheongsam, and then he took me to East Hampton for some exterior beach shots. At one point, he placed me near a backdrop of shrubbery so I could look like I was communing with nature. Two days later, my face and arms were covered with an angry, itchy red rash. Bert showed a picture of the "shrubbery" to a horticulturist, who confirmed that the pretty green backdrop was poison ivy. I had never been exposed to it before, so my case was severe. It was hardly the glamorous life of a young movie star, but even the story of my rash was reported in the gossip columns.

Life selected a photograph of me wearing my cheongsam for the October 24, 1960, cover. I'm staring straight at the camera, looking both innocent and knowing, wearing a form-fitting silk dress with a high neck and a leg-revealing slit. I grew up wearing cheongsams custom-made by Hong Kong tailors in an endless variety of jewel-toned silks. They were sewn quickly and priced reasonably. Women and girls of all ages had them for every occasion, and they were always in style. But they were a novelty in America, and Suzie Wong started a fashion trend.

After creating my red cheongsam-like dress for the Stark's "East meets West" party, designer Guy LaRoche was inspired to include similar dresses—fitted, high-necked sheaths with a slit on the side—in his new Paris collection. Suzy Perette, a New York garment manufacturer, rushed *their* version of the cheongsam into production when *Suzie Wong* came out, predicting that American women would want to dress just like Nancy Kwan. Suddenly, I saw my signature Hong Kong look everywhere.

Premieres were planned in London and Los Angeles. Ray's original list included a Hong Kong premiere, but he told the press that he abandoned the idea because some factions in the city protested that *Suzie Wong*'s Hollywood portrayal of prostitutes and the red-light district attracted the wrong kind of tourists to the wrong part of town. While that attitude was not widely held, the negative publicity convinced Ray to concentrate on more welcoming cities.

The London premiere was significant to me because I was accompanied by my father, Aunty Nan, and Granny May. They were excited to see my screen debut and experience everything that went with it—the red carpet lined with photographers eager to take our picture, the theater filled with celebrities, the hush when the lights went down, the applause at the end, the after-party—I was thrilled to share these moments with them. I'm sure some of the scenes in the film were difficult for my very proper father to watch, but he was a sophisticated and open-minded man who could separate his daughter from her controversial role. Daddy and Aunty Nan also accompanied me to the premiere in Hollywood at Grauman's Chinese Theatre.

The World of Suzie Wong was a box-office hit, and critics were enthusiastic about my performance. Bosley Crowther of the *New York Times* wrote that the film was "wildly romantic" and "vividly imagined" and seemed charmed by my portrayal of Suzie. He said, "A new girl named Nancy Kwan plays her so blithely and innocently that even the ladies should love her."

Favorable reviews were nice, but Ray Stark's confidence in me after my screen debut was empowering. He was my biggest fan. Kirk Douglas once said, "If Ray believes in you, he'll put all his wizardry at your command and make it happen." To Ray's credit, he didn't think of me as an Asian actress but saw me as "a girl of many nations, packaged on one body...an Italian girl—or an American girl, a French girl, or an English girl," and cast a wide net while considering my next role.

Ironically—and unexpectedly—a wonderful opportunity came to me because I *was* Asian. I was at one of those Holly-wood parties that young actresses are encouraged to attend so they can be seen by the right people, especially producers who might be casting a role. Usually, I'm shy and uncomfortable at these events, but on that night, I was with some friends and enjoying myself.

Suddenly, a man rushed over to me and said, "Linda Low!" *Who the hell is that?* I thought. Was he trying to pick me up? Then he exclaimed, "You're perfect! You're my Linda Low."

Who is this man? Is he for real?

He was very real. He was Ross Hunter, the hottest producer in Hollywood because his last six movies—including *Magnificent Obsession, All That Heaven Allows, Imitation of Life*, and most recently, *Midnight Lace*—were big hits that had grossed a whop-ping $53,000,000. Ross was a showman, and his success was fueled by his belief that movies should be pure entertainment— that people wanted to get away from the grim side of life. He famously said, "If people wanted to meet the girl next door, they'd go next door." His philosophy was "Entertainment through beauty—beautiful women in beautiful clothes in beau-tiful sets," and audiences loved his glamorous films that featured big box office stars and dramatic plots.

His new project was a film version of Rodgers and Hammer-stein's Broadway musical *Flower Drum Song*, and he wanted me to play Linda, the singing and dancing spitfire who stole the show on Broadway. "You'll be hearing from me," he promised. I was flabbergasted and very flattered.

When I learned more about the show, I couldn't imagine a better role than Linda Low. She loved to dance (just like me). She was independent and outspoken (also just like me!). She had an active fantasy life and was intelligent, playful, and liked to have fun. And as the Rodgers and Hammerstein hit song said, she enjoyed being a girl. Maybe she was a little bold, and I remember thinking, "Oh my God! What will the Asians think of this?" But that was the best thing about Linda—she wasn't stereotypically Asian. She was just the opposite, a modern girl who could have been of any nationality.

Did I want the part? Yes!

Ross called immediately after he saw me at the party. It was the easiest role I ever won.

I was in the second year of my seven-year contract with Seven Arts, so the company had to set up a loan-out agreement enabling me to work for Ross. It was a common practice at the time. Actors under contract had no autonomy. We were commodities, traded back and forth, depending on where we were wanted or needed, and if we refused, we were placed on suspension without salary. Unlike some actors, I was happy with the arrangement because I was young, inexperienced, and grateful to have Ray Stark looking out for me. After the success of *Suzie Wong*, I received many offers.

I was offered *Kitten with a Whip* (which Ann-Margret ended up doing) and *A Candle for St. Jude*, based on a book by Rumer Godden. I loved the story of *A Candle for St. Jude* because it was set in a ballet school, and I knew that world, but it was a small project that would take time to pull together. Meanwhile, Ross

Hunter was fast-tracking production on *Flower Drum Song*, and I relied on Ray to make the deal.

Saying yes to one film means saying no to others. Because I had signed to play Linda Low, I had to pass on an offer from the most popular entertainer in the world.

I was told that a producer wanted to discuss a new project and would meet me at a studio soundstage. I arrived at the appointed hour and waited, then a door opened. Elvis Presley and his entourage walked into the vast room. "I'm Elvis Presley," he said (as if he needed an introduction). "May I sing you a song from my next film, *Blue Hawaii*?" I sat in a chair and listened, spellbound, while the King of Rock and Roll serenaded me. When he finished, I jumped up and applauded.

Did that really happen?

Elvis wanted me to be his love interest in *Blue Hawaii*, but I had to decline because of my previous commitment to *Flower Drum Song*. To this day, I still can't believe I said no to Elvis Presley!

CHAPTER 7

I didn't see the stage production of *Flower Drum Song* while working on Broadway, but I had friends in the show and was familiar with the story. It was based on the novel *The Flower Drum Song* by Chin Y. Lee, a young journalist who escaped from China during World War II and studied at Yale. He moved to San Francisco's Chinatown, where he lived above a nightclub, and supported himself by writing a column for a local newspaper. His passion project was his novel, a story about interconnected lives in contemporary Chinatown, but every major publisher rejected it.

Lee was broke, discouraged, and didn't know how he would pay for his next meal. Then, a miracle. An elderly reader who evaluated manuscripts for the publisher Farrar, Straus was on his deathbed when he read *The Flower Drum Song*, but he scribbled the words "Read this" on Lee's manuscript right before he passed away. Editor John Farrar took the dying man's recommendation seriously and published the novel in 1957. It became a bestseller. Readers were charmed by Lee's story about the "What are we going to do about the younger generation?" conflict between old-world parents and their new-world children. In the 1950s, everyone was experiencing the *Rebel Without a Cause* clash between teenagers and their elders. Lee's story of an Asian family's attempt to bridge the generational divide between traditional and contemporary values seemed highly relatable.

The novel caught the attention of Richard Rodgers and Oscar Hammerstein, whose hit musical *South Pacific* also featured Asian characters. They wrote and produced *Flower Drum Song* for the stage in 1958. Directed by Gene Kelly, the show ran for over six hundred performances. Pat Suzuki, who played Linda Low, was celebrated for her performance of the show's hit song, "I Enjoy Being a Girl." Her co-star Miyoshi Umeki, who played the ingenue Mei Li in the show, made history that year when she received an Academy Award for Best Supporting Actress for her performance in *Sayonara* because she was the first Asian actor to win an Oscar. Both women appeared on the cover of *Time* magazine.

The show was a hot property. Ross Hunter was so convinced that a movie version would have universal appeal that he paid a million dollars for the film rights. Although set in San Francisco's Chinatown, *Flower Drum Song* could be about any immigrant family trying to bridge the generation gap. On top of that, it had romance, comedy, and a sensational score.

The story begins with Mei Li, a young Chinese woman, and her father, Dr. Li, who travel from China to San Francisco as stowaways because the Fong family has invited her to be their son Sammy's "picture bride." Sammy, a hipster who owns the Celestial Garden, a popular Chinatown nightclub, has no intention of honoring the marriage contract because he is in love with Linda Low, the showgirl who is the headliner at his club. He brings Mei Li and her father to Wang Chi-Yang, a patriarch who wants his son Ta to settle down with a respectable bride. Wang battles with Ta (and with his younger son, Wang San) because his old-world beliefs are at odds with the modern ideas of the younger generation.

Ironically, Ta and Mei Li are instantly attracted to each other. Then, Ta is momentarily dazzled by the irresistible Linda, who conceals her profession and seduces him into proposing marriage as a ploy to make Sammy jealous. Sammy retaliates by inviting Wang and his family to the club, where they are shocked to see Linda performing onstage.

Sammy decides he's had enough of bachelorhood and proposes to Linda, while Ta convinces Mei Li that he loves *her*. But the star-crossed couples are thwarted by the picture bride contract, a binding document in Chinatown. On the day she is supposed to marry Sammy, Mei Li comes up with a clever solution she saw in an old movie. She tells Sammy's mother that the contract is invalid because she entered the country illegally. In a wildly romantic finale that could only happen in a musical, she marries Ta, Sammy marries Linda, and everyone lives happily ever after.

Ross set up the project at Universal, secured a $5 million budget, and announced that *Flower Drum Song* would be Hollywood's first major production featuring an all-Asian cast.

I didn't understand the significance of Ross's decision to make an all-Asian film until I met the cast. They were so excited and proud to be part of this historic project. Benson Fong, who was set to play Wang Chi-Yang, the patriarch who is constantly exasperated by the behavior of his Americanized sons, explained *why* the project was significant. He told me that if I looked at American film history, I would not find a single film with an all-Asian cast. Instead, I'd see Caucasians dressed up as Asians and made up in yellowface.

I had seen enough Hollywood movies to understand that if a story called for an Asian hero or a heroine, the part typically went to a white actor who was transformed with elaborate makeup. Using pigments, tape, rubber bands, and prosthetics, makeup artists created the illusion of yellow skin, hooded eyes, and other Asian features. In 1956's *Teahouse of the August Moon*, Marlon Brando was fitted with facial prosthetics to play a Japanese interpreter. German-born Luise Rainer played a Chinese farmer in *The Good Earth* in 1937 and won the Academy Award for her performance. John Wayne played Genghis Kahn. In a reversal, *The World of Suzie Wong*'s makeup artists had to make me look *more* Asian by covering my freckles with foundation and thinning my eyebrows.

Because I grew up in Hong Kong and went to school in England, I wasn't familiar with the history of how Asians were treated in America and marginalized in Hollywood, but as I became more knowledgeable, I realized what Benson said was true.

Asian Americans had been held back by long-standing prejudicial forces working against them. Chinese workers came to America to build the country's railroads, but the Chinese Exclusion Act of 1882 restricted Chinese (and subsequently *all* Asian) immigration for the next sixty years. Bigotry against Asian Americans, who were historically maligned as the "Yellow Peril," intensified during times of national distress, notably after the bombing of Pearl Harbor in 1941, when FDR signed Executive Order 9066, which led to the incarceration of 120,000 Japanese Americans in internment camps.

Meanwhile, Hollywood had its own set of exclusionary rules. The Hays Code, "guidelines" for films released between 1934

and 1968, prohibited nudity, sexual perversion, drug trafficking, ridicule of the clergy, scenes of childbirth, white slavery, profanity, and miscegenation, meaning depictions of interracial relationships. Through the late 1940s, interracial marriage was banned in thirty states (Alabama had a law on the books as late as 2000). Enforcement of the Hays Code prevented Blacks and Asians from playing romantic leads opposite Caucasians, ensuring Hollywood would not offend potential ticket buyers by showing them interracial love scenes.

Barred from leading roles, Asian actors had few options. They were cast as Fu Manchu villains, hypersexualized Dragon Ladies, and comic buffoons, or appeared in minor roles as shopkeepers, maids, and houseboys. When I arrived in Hollywood, only two talent agents represented Asian clients, and most of their work consisted of finding extras for crowd scenes. Though the Hays Code started to lose its power in the 1950s, by that time, Asian actors had been denied viable careers for generations.

Many of my fellow cast members in *Flower Drum Song* had experienced prejudice firsthand. Jack Soo, set to play nightclub owner Sammy Fong (the role he performed so brilliantly in the Broadway production), was Japanese and grew up in California, where he graduated from Berkeley with a degree in English. Yet, like thousands of Japanese Americans, he was placed in an internment camp during World War II and subsequently had to change his name from Suzuki to Soo to avoid being the target of widespread prejudice against the Japanese.

James Shigeta, slated to be *Flower Drum Song*'s romantic lead, Wang Ta, was born in Hawaii and was a multitalented (and extremely handsome) actor and singer who became known as the "Frank Sinatra of Japan" early in his career. He starred

in Samuel Fuller's provocative noir drama *The Crimson Kimono* in 1959—provocative because James was one of the first Asian Americans to play a romantic lead—a Japanese American police detective who competes with his white partner for the affection of a blonde ingenue. The film exploited this explosive love triangle with the tagline, *"Yes, this is a beautiful American girl in the arms of a Japanese boy! What was his strange appeal for American girls?"* Notably (and atypically), James's character got the girl in the end.

He won the Golden Globe for Most Promising Newcomer in 1960 and seemed to have a bright career ahead of him, yet a movie executive told him that his race was holding him back. "If you were white," the executive explained, "you'd be a hell of a big star."

On a personal note, when my good friend Irene Tsu was cast as a dancer in *Flower Drum Song* and needed a new place to live, she asked to see a vacant apartment in Beverly Hills. The landlord told her, "We don't have any Asians here." She solved that problem by moving in with me.

These stories were disturbing, but the one that broke my heart was the sad saga of the rise and fall of Anna May Wong. I first learned about her when I started working in Hollywood. Then, Ross Hunter told me that he had cast her in *Flower Drum Song*, a bold and big-hearted move on his part because Wong, who had starred in over sixty films during her long career and was celebrated as a great actress and a style icon, had fallen on hard times in her later years. In 1960, she had a small part in Ross's film *Portrait in Black*, starring Lana Turner and Anthony Quinn. Ross greatly respected her talent and knew she would be perfect as Madame Liang, the outspoken and civic-minded matriarch

in *Flower Drum Song*. The more I heard about Wong, the more excited I was about working with this legendary actress.

I couldn't see her work because her films from the Silent Era weren't available for viewing the way they are now, but I found her story fascinating. She was born Wong Liu Tsong in Los Angeles's Chinatown, where her family owned and operated a laundry. She appeared as an extra in one of D. W. Griffith's films and then started getting small roles in silent films. Unfortunately, when Wong began her career, only Caucasian actors were cast in lead roles that required the character to be Asian. Her acclaimed performance in Douglas Fairbanks's *The Thief of Bagdad* should have made her a bona fide Hollywood star. Instead, she remained a supporting player. She reinvented herself by moving to Europe in the late 1920s, where she found wider acceptance and was offered starring roles in films. She also appeared on the London stage in *Picadilly*, *The Chalk Circle*, and several musical reviews.

In 1931, Wong starred as the seductive daughter of Dr. Fu Manchu in *Daughter of the Dragon*, playing opposite Sessue Hayakawa, who also had a storied career in Hollywood. The son of wealthy parents who imagined a career in banking for their brilliant son, Hayakawa studied at the University of Chicago, then moved to Los Angeles, where he discovered he had a talent for acting and won a leading role in *The Typhoon* in 1914 and *The Cheat* in 1915. American women swooned over Hayakawa's brooding good looks and embraced him as a matinee idol. He played the forbidden lover in popular silent films and became one of the highest-paid actors in Hollywood until the 1920s when a new wave of anti-Asian sentiment surfaced.

In 1924, the American government responded to concerns about the impact of increased immigration numbers on the social and demographic profile of the country. To keep America *American*, Congress passed the Immigration Act of 1924, also known as the Johnson-Reed Act, that prevented *all* immigration from Asia and set quotas on the number of immigrants allowed from Eastern and Southern Europe. After enjoying so much success, Hayakawa found limited opportunities in Hollywood and, like Anna May Wong, moved abroad to work. *Daughter of the Dragon* revitalized his career, and he won an Academy Award nomination in 1957 for his work in *The Bridge on the River Kwai*.

Wong was lauded for her performance in *Daughter of the Dragon* and became an international celebrity. More than anything, she wanted to play the role of O-Lan in the 1937 film adaptation of Pearl Buck's novel *The Good Earth*. Instead, MGM passed her over for Luise Rainer, who won the Academy Award for Best Actress for her performance. I can't imagine how Anna May Wong must have felt. I would have quit show business.

I admire Anna May Wong's tenacity and determination to achieve her goals, and I could see many connections between our stories. In 1938, she appeared on the cover of *Look* magazine with the tagline "The World's Most Beautiful Chinese Girl," which reminded me of my *Life* magazine cover. She was considered a fashion icon, and her ability to turn classic Chinese designs into mainstream fashion trends was similar to my cheongsam's impact on American women, inspiring them to dress like me.

Wong had family in Hong Kong and traveled to China for the first time in 1936. She found many friends and supporters there, but the Chinese government was hostile because of her Dragon Lady/temptress roles and banned some of her films.

Madame Chiang Kai-shek, the First Lady of the Republic of China and a Wellesley College graduate, disliked Hollywood's presentation of Chinese characters in films. In her mind, Anna May Wong embodied the stereotypes she disdained. Wong was low class (her family was Cantonese, not Mandarin), and the roles she played, whether a maid or a siren, were undignified, the worst kind of Chinese.

Though Wong worked tirelessly to raise money for the United China Relief fund during World War II, she was publicly snubbed by Madame Chiang Kai-shek when the first lady gave a much-publicized speech at the Hollywood Bowl during her six-week goodwill tour of America in 1943. Thirty thousand people attended to show their support for China, and many white celebrities joined the first lady on the stage. But Wong, arguably the most famous Asian actress in the world, was not invited because Madame Chiang Kai-shek thought she wasn't good enough.

Wong's detractors confused her with the roles she played, often the roles she *had* to play because they were the only ones offered to her. Should she have turned down opportunities even though she wanted—and needed—to work?

There were times when I was subject to the same kind of prejudice, like when the clueless interviewer criticized me for playing a prostitute, and journalists erased my command of English in their articles. I imagine Madame Chiang Kai-shek would have been equally harsh and unforgiving to me as she was with Anna May Wong.

I never had the opportunity to meet Anna May Wong because she died of a heart attack right before we were scheduled to start filming. She was found in bed with the *Flower Drum Song* script by her side. Decades of heavy drinking—and disappointments— had taken their toll. It was tragic that audiences were denied the opportunity to see this remarkable actress in a role that would have made her famous again. I'm happy that recent biographies and film retrospectives have reacquainted the world with her accomplishments.

Learning these stories (and I continue to learn) was a valuable part of my education. When I came to Hollywood, I was backed by a studio and powerful people in the film business, so I was spared the experiences other Asian actors endured. Now, along with my fellow *Flower Drum Song* cast members, I hoped the film would open doors for all Asian actors and give Asian audiences the rare opportunity to see themselves reflected on-screen. It was 1961, for goodness' sake, and about time.

CHAPTER 8

Flower Drum Song was Ross Hunter's first musical and most ambitious project, but he had every imaginable resource at his disposal because he was Hollywood's box office king. Boyish and bespectacled, thirty-seven-year-old Ross looked like a high school English teacher, which was his profession after he graduated from college—until he decided to become an actor and went on to play heartthrobs in B pictures. A year-long illness derailed his screen career, prompting him to reinvent himself as a production executive and then a producer.

Ross evolved into a flamboyant showman who seemed to know exactly what audiences wanted. Bucking the new trend of realistic movies with depressing backgrounds and characters he dismissed as "grubby," Ross produced films with strong, often melodramatic stories, opulent sets, and, whenever possible, beautiful women dressed in furs. His ambition was "to bring Hollywood back to Hollywood."

His formula worked, and many blockbusters (and millions of dollars in ticket sales) later, Ross ruled the Universal lot from a luxurious "bungalow" that was larger than the average home. Like the glamorous sets in his movies, his bungalow had five rooms with plush white carpeting (a bold choice considering that his dog, Archie, frequently accompanied him to work), sleek black leather furniture, and white walls hung with valuable works of art. From this luxurious perch, Ross oversaw every detail of the production.

He rounded out the cast with Myoshi Umecki as Mei Li, reprising the role she created on Broadway. He also hired Juanita Hall, the first African American to win a Tony Award (Best Supporting Actress for her role as Bloody Mary in *South Pacific*), to replace Anna May Wong as Madame Liang. And he cast Reiko Sato, an actress and a beautiful dancer, to play the character Helen Chao.

Ross assembled a team of award-winning professionals to bring his extravagant vision of the stage musical to life. "Award-winning" is a bit of an understatement. Ross's production team had been honored with a collective seventy-nine Academy Award nominations and thirteen wins and would receive many more nominations and awards in the future.

Director Henry Koster was a veteran filmmaker with a substantial list of credits. A fugitive from Nazi Germany in the 1930s, the young filmmaker emigrated to Hollywood and made his very first film at Universal. *Three Smart Girls*, starring teenage Deanna Durbin, was so successful that it saved the studio from bankruptcy. Koster worked with Hollywood A-listers and went on to direct Loretta Young in *The Bishop's Wife*, Jimmy Stewart in *Harvey*, Olivia de Havilland and Richard Burton in *My Cousin Rachel*, Marlon Brando in *Désirée*, and Ava Gardner in *The Naked Maja*.

Henry was a solid director *and* a good husband. He promised his wife, Peggy, an actress, that there would always be a place for her in his films. When he couldn't cast the real-life Peggy, he whimsically displayed a statue of her somewhere on the set—so she was visible even when she wasn't there in the flesh. In *Flower Drum Song*, Peggy's lovely face can be seen on a bust sitting atop a television.

Russell Metty was a versatile cinematographer who had worked with many legendary directors, including Douglas Sirk, Orson Welles, and John Huston. He was known for his edgy black-and-white images and dramatic use of technicolor, which was key to the lush, oversaturated look of every Ross Hunter production, where the sets and costumes were as important as the actors.

For the showstopping costumes Ross envisioned, he selected Irene Sharaff, who created the costumes for the original Broadway production of *Flower Drum Song* and the films *The King and I, Brigadoon*, and *An American in Paris*. Like Edith Head, she was always in demand because she had a great sense of style and an unerring talent for expressing character through one-of-a-kind costumes that were original, imaginative, and inspired by meticulous research.

But Henry's most inspired hire was Hermes Pan, the film's choreographer. Known as "the man who danced with Fred Astaire," Hermes had a lifelong collaboration with the legendary Astaire and other stars, including Ginger Rogers, Betty Grable, Judy Garland, Rita Hayworth, Ann Miller, and Cyd Charisse during the golden age of Hollywood musicals. I had seen all his films, and dance was still my first love, so I couldn't wait to work with him.

We started rehearsing in February. When I reported to work at Universal Studios, I felt as if I had been transported to fantasyland. Everywhere I looked, I saw monuments to Hollywood history: Alfred Hitchcock's sinister *Psycho* house; Spartacus Square, the setting for sword and sandal epics; Western streets where gunslingers staged showdowns; the European courtyard that doubled for any old-world location; Park Lake, the lair of the Creature from the Black Lagoon, Old New York, Main Street USA, and other iconic sets.

Costumed actors and extras roamed the busy lot. Stars dined at the commissary, better known for its networking opportunities than its menu. Side streets held rows of small dressing rooms for supporting players and larger bungalows and trailers for stars, directors, and producers. The studio even had its own post office and medical facilities. It was a sprawling, self-sufficient city dedicated to making movie magic.

Ross was famous for pampering his leading ladies. When he discovered that Doris Day had a passion for candied fruit, he delivered a fresh batch to her dressing room every day. He thoughtfully outfitted my trailer with air-conditioning, a kitchen, and even a hi-fi if I wanted to listen to music. And he welcomed me with an extravagant bouquet of white roses. Ross usually sent dozens of red roses to his leading lady when a picture started, but someone told him that white meant good luck in China, so he sent a special arrangement to me. I didn't have the heart to tell him *red* signifies good luck in China while white is usually associated with death. It was the thought that counted, and I appreciated the gesture.

Stage 12, the largest one on the Universal lot, would be *Flower Drum Song*'s home for several months. From the outside, it looked like a giant warehouse. Inside, studio workers busily constructed a replica of Grant Avenue in San Francisco's Chinatown, the largest and costliest set built on a Hollywood soundstage. The set was *so* large (51,300 square feet) that Stage 12 had to be extended to accommodate nine additional Chinatown buildings.

Why not use the real Grant Avenue? Studio accountants determined that building a $310,000 set would be less expensive than transporting the film's cast and crew to Chinatown for an entire month, the time needed to shoot a pivotal musical number that featured a parade with two thousand extras and a marching band.

Preproduction was intense and began with six weeks of dance rehearsals. When I first met Hermes, he knew I was a ballet dancer, but he needed to figure out how much jazz or modern dance I'd done. We talked, then moved to the dance floor. It was like one of those magical Fred and Ginger moments when the characters get to know each other while dancing together. Hermes showed me what he had in mind. "This is the feel I want for 'Grant Avenue,'" he'd say, demonstrating the steps and stopping to ask if I could manage them. I was a little nervous and had to keep reminding myself *not* to turn out my feet in a classic ballerina stance. And I found it a little intimidating that the choreographer who worked with Ginger Rogers and other great dancers was now dancing with me.

Fortunately, my muscle memory kicked in, and I adapted quickly. Hermes was a kind, soft-spoken teacher committed to helping me—and everyone else—do their best. He was so impressed by young Patrick Adiarte, who played teenage Wang San onstage and was reprising his role for the film, that he gave him more and more to do. He was generous that way.

The most disconcerting thing about Hermes was that he looked so much like Fred Astaire. People always noted the resemblance between the two lean, elegant men. They were about the same height and moved similarly—they could have been brothers! I saw it myself one day in the rehearsal room. Our eyes were always on the mirror when we danced because we had to watch ourselves and everybody else to stay in sync. I was checking myself in the mirror when I saw Hermes by the piano, where he usually stood. Then I turned and looked again. I couldn't believe what I was seeing. It wasn't Hermes, it was Fred Astaire!

Fred Astaire had come to watch us dance!

I almost missed a step. Then, all the dancers noticed him at the exact moment, and a ripple of excitement went through the room. Luckily, the shock didn't send us crashing into each other. We were freaking out on the inside (Fred Astaire!!!). Thank God we had been practicing the number for weeks, so we could calm down and show off a little. Hermes introduced us to the maestro, and Fred was gracious and complimentary; his praise meant so much to us.

I had the opportunity to get to know Fred better when Hermes brought me to his home in Beverly Hills for chatty visits. The house was unassuming from the outside—a mid-century modern that Fred had built on land formerly a part of Mary Pickford's Pickfair estate. But the interior was just like Fred—elegant, comfortable, and beautifully put together. I was content to sit with the two gentlemen and listen to their stories about the musicals and dances they'd created together. At Fred's, movie history came to life.

While I rehearsed the dances, I studied the script. It was a process: Learn the steps, memorize my lines and songs, and then put it all together in a way that was supposed to look spontaneous and effortless. I had hoped to do my singing in the film, but Universal preferred to dub actors with professionals who specialized in movie voice-overs so the sound would be easier to control. James Shigeta and Miyoshi were the exceptions because they had been famous singers with hit records.

Most studios hired "ghost singers." Marni Nixon, who sang for Deborah Kerr in *The King and I* and Audrey Hepburn in *My Fair Lady*, was in constant demand. As skilled as she was, Nixon had an operatic voice that came across as grand and old-fashioned. Ross wanted Linda Low to sound fresher, more contemporary, and *jazzier*. B. J. Baker was all of that. Once married to Mickey Rooney, she was a backup singer who recorded with Elvis, Frank Sinatra, and Bobby Darin and performed with the Anita Kerr singers. When B. J. sang my songs, her voice was youthful and flirtatious, *exactly* how Linda Low should sound.

During preproduction, we finalized my costumes, hair, and makeup. My fittings with Irene Sharaff taught me so much about the art of costume design. Irene was a formidable woman who took her work very seriously. A dress was never just a dress. She had a process when she conceived a costume. "First, I sketch the character as I envision him or her from the script," Sharaff explained in an interview. "Then, after meeting with the star, I will modify the concept to fit the personality of the actor or actress." She studied the actors, looking for strengths to emphasize and weaknesses to hide, and she knew how to make the clothes look good on film, which meant selecting the right fabrics and adjusting the color so it would register appropriately on camera.

It wasn't enough for *me* to look good. My costume had to relate to the other characters and the sets. For the scene where I meet Ta's family for the first time, and I'm pretending to be the kind of good girl a young man brings home to meet his father, Irene dressed me in a classic cheongsam...but with a twist. Its bright gold color was meant to stand out from the pastel party dresses worn by the other women, but it was skintight, with a high slit. The dress communicated everything about Linda Low in that scene: she was demure but still undeniably *hot*.

When Irene showed me my costumes, I realized that the look, however beautiful, was just the starting point. Each garment had been designed with movement in mind. A dancer uses her body to express herself, whether she walks across a room or performs on a stage. My costumes had to be constructed to allow that freedom of movement, which requires a fundamental understanding of how dancers use their bodies. My costumes were tight to accentuate my figure but fluid in all the right places. Irene knew how to make that happen.

There was one time when I questioned one of Irene's bold choices. She placed a bright pink pom-pom on my head for one of my scenes. I looked at this strange thing, wondering how it would stay on my head, and said, "Irene?!!" "No, it's great," she assured me. "It gives her that *touch*," and she was absolutely right. The pom-pom suggested I was a girl who was a little kookie, didn't take herself seriously, and knew how to have fun. Years later, a friend told me the funny hat had come up for sale at auction—I couldn't believe someone saved it for all those years! I wish I had.

And because this was a Ross Hunter production, there had to be that touch of mink, the ultimate expression of a leading lady's elevated status. Who knows how Linda Low could afford to drape herself in fur, but she looked glamorous and expensive. The fantasy was always more important to Ross than the reality.

I got along beautifully with Ross, except when we argued about how I would wear my waist-length hair. When I reported for work, he made a suggestion that sounded more like an order. "Cut it." He thought a bob would make Linda look more contemporary.

"*I will not*," I said defiantly. I thought Linda should have long, swinging hair and nothing he could say would change my mind. But I had an idea. I went to see Larry Germain and Bud Westmore, the department heads responsible for hair and makeup and asked if I could try on a wig. They found one in the archives and styled it for me. Then, I marched over to Ross's office to show him my new hairstyle.

He was happily surprised. "You look absolutely beautiful," he gushed. "I'm sorry you had to cut it, but I appreciate it. You're a doll."

"I'm a smart doll," I said as I pulled off the wig.

Fortunately, Ross had a sense of humor. We compromised, and I wore the wig in one scene—we didn't have to explain *why* Linda's hair was suddenly shorter. It was Hollywood!

I don't remember having unusually long makeup sessions, but Miyoshi complained that she had to show up at 6 a.m., long before everyone else, and sit in the chair for two hours. Because she was Japanese, special makeup had to be applied every morning to make her look more Chinese. At the other end of Hollywood, one of the unanticipated results of *Flower Drum Song*'s enormous all-Asian cast was that other studios had no actors or extras to play Asians in their movies. Makeup artists complained that they had to go back to using the yellowface technique to make white actors look Asian the whole time *Flower Drum Song* was shooting.

I had several big dance numbers in the movie, and one was a striptease at Sammy Fong's Celestial Garden nightclub. "Fan Tan Fannie" would be a pretty tame striptease because I wouldn't take anything off. Still, the dance number had to be suggestive enough to shock Wang Chi-Yang, Benson Fong's character, who is surprised to see his son's fiancée performing brazenly onstage. Ross was so committed to accuracy that he scheduled a real stripper to teach me how to do it convincingly. Then, he watched a rehearsal and saw that my Royal Ballet training was so comprehensive that it prepared me for "exotic" dancing. Ross liked every move and canceled the stripper's tutorial.

When I asked Irene Sharaff what costume she had in mind for "Fan Tan Fannie," she said, "Fans!" and pulled out a storyboard to show how I would cover—and uncover—my feminine charms with fans, a technique that had been around since Sally Rand performed burlesque in the 1930s. But Ross wanted the audience to see something new and different, she explained, so they came up with a "high-tech" version of a classic striptease by commissioning an aviation engineer to design decorative fans powered by tiny motors. The mechanisms were attached to my bosom and waist with wires. When it was time for the big reveal, I pushed a button to make the fans magically snap shut, and my costumed top and bottom (nothing more than that) would suddenly be on display.

Word got around fast. The day we filmed the fan dance, over two hundred visitors came to the set to see this marvel of modern science. Henry joked that it was amazing what a crowd those little motors could attract. Everyone was hoping for a major wardrobe malfunction, but the fans worked perfectly, and we did it in one take!

While "Fan Tan Fannie" had technical challenges, "I Enjoy Being a Girl" was a cinematic tour de force. I had to "sing" and dance in front of a large, three-way mirror. At various moments during the number, my reflections would take on a life of their own and model different outfits—a fur stole, a gown, a frilly dress—while I was still wearing my slip.

Today, computer-generated imaging can achieve this effect in seconds. Back then, it was a complicated process that depended on specific camera placement and limited movement within a narrow field. I had to act, dance, mime the song, stay within my marks, take directions, *and* remember the cinematographer's long list of instructions. "Don't put your hand out too far." "When you pirouette, come back to the same place." "Make sure you're looking at the right mirror." "Smile!" And I had to do all this while wearing a barely there silk slip, about an inch away from being immodest.

It was going to be a long day. Maybe two. My youth was my superpower because I had the energy and the stamina to keep going.

At some point during the shoot, I looked in the mirror and saw a man walking by. But he wasn't just any man. He was Cary Grant, a vision who would challenge *anyone's* concentration. We didn't meet that day, but Cary returned to the set to pose for publicity shots. When a reporter asked me how I felt about having my picture taken with the legendary actor, I was completely honest. "I'll never do that again," I told him. "Mr. Grant knows all the tricks, and he's too beautiful. Next to him, I look ugly!"

After that first Cary Grant sighting, "I Enjoy Being a Girl" took hours to complete, and I felt like I had finished a marathon when Henry Koster finally said, "Cut." The crew applauded spontaneously, which acknowledged how hard it had been to film the scene, and I went home to the apartment I shared with my friend, Irene Tsu.

My phone rang later that night. Ross was calling with terrible news. Everything was perfect when they looked at the dailies, the footage we had shot that day. Well, almost everything. "Nancy, we have to reshoot the scene," he said. A fly had gotten into the camera's gate and was visible in every carefully designed shot.

The next day, we did the whole scene again. At that point, I wasn't so sure I enjoyed being a girl.

CHAPTER 9

In addition to filming *Flower Drum Song*, I was still doing publicity for *The World of Suzie Wong*. On top of that, I was named New Star of the Year by the Hollywood Foreign Press Association and nominated for Best Actress in a Motion Picture Drama, an award to be given at their annual Golden Globes ceremony. When I saw the names of the other nominees in the category, Elizabeth Taylor in *Butterfield 8*, Jean Simmons in *Elmer Gantry*, Doris Day in *Midnight Lace* (a Ross Hunter film), and Greer Garson in *Sunrise at Campobello*—I thought I must be dreaming. I don't remember much about the night except that Greer Garson won, and I was thrilled to be in the company of such great actresses.

Whenever I had a break from shooting, I walked over to the set of *Judgment at Nuremberg* to watch Spencer Tracy, my favorite actor, at work. *Judgment at Nuremberg* was a weighty drama about the trial of Nazi war criminals, with Spencer Tracy playing the judge who has the difficult job of determining the guilt or innocence of the four German defendants. I say difficult because the young German lawyer representing the accused presents a complex—and at times, compelling—defense suggesting that the whole *world* was complicit in Hitler's crimes.

I watched the film recently and was impressed by how provocative and prophetic it was as it charted a dictator's rise to power and his ability to exploit weaknesses in human nature. The film is in black and white, which ties it to the past, but the acting is superb, and there's nothing dated about the story, which seems especially relevant today.

I loved to stand in the back and observe the actors. While I was watching them, one was watching *me*—Maximilian Schell, the young actor playing the firebrand German lawyer. He kept looking in my direction. Born in Austria, Max was a man of many talents who thought he'd become a painter, a musician, or a playwright but eventually fell in love with acting. His sister was the acclaimed actress Maria Schell.

Max had made several films in Europe, including a German production of *Hamlet*. Critics loved it, calling him one of the greatest Hamlets ever. Hollywood took notice, and he was offered roles in American films.

Max perfected his English while filming *The Young Lions* with Marlon Brando. Then he played lawyer Hans Rolfe in the Playhouse 90 television production of *Judgment at Nuremberg*, winning the attention of producer/director Stanley Kramer, who cast him in the feature film version.

Whenever Max performed in a scene, all eyes were on him, which says a lot because his co-stars—Spencer Tracy, Burt Lancaster, Marlene Dietrich, Montgomery Cliff, Judy Garland, and Richard Widmark—were screen legends. In addition to being a fine actor, Max was extraordinarily handsome—six feet tall, with dark hair and intense eyes. He was charismatic, like a more mature Warren Beatty. But his passion and fierce intelligence were even more compelling than his powerful physical presence.

During one of my visits to the set, Max introduced himself, and later, we ran into each other at a party hosted by Henry Koster. We felt a connection, an undeniable attraction. And that was it. Lunch led to dinner, dinner to romance, and suddenly, we were a couple, which, as I discovered, had an entirely different meaning in Hollywood. When an actor dates another actor, gossip columnists seize upon the relationship and spin it into a continuing drama. If we went to a party at Ray Stark's or dinner at Benson Fong's restaurant, Ah Fong, the sighting would be reported in the newspapers the following day. We went from "hello" to *WILL HE MARRY HER?* in record time.

Max maintained his cool with the press. More often than not, he'd tell reporters, "I don't discuss my personal life." But that didn't stop them from printing wildly inaccurate stories about our alleged escapades, imagined fights, and reputedly opposing ideas about marriage. According to the columns, I was eager to wed, but Max was a free spirit with no intention of settling down. Soon after we met, a reporter wrote that I was bringing Max home to Hong Kong to meet my father (part of my alleged campaign to get him to propose). None of it was true, but the studio loved it because it kept our names—and their films—in the headlines.

I was so tired of reading these fabrications that when popular columnist Joe Hyams interviewed me, I said, "I'll tell you a secret. All those funny things I'm supposed to have said: they were made up in advance by the press agent on the film." He looked at me incredulously, probably thinking, *who admits that to a reporter?* Then I said, "And if I don't say the things you want me to, then make them up for me . . . that's what most newspapermen do." Unlike other actresses being groomed for success by the studio, I didn't play by the rules. Some people found my candor refreshing.

If Hedda Hopper and Luella Parsons—the legendary gossip columnists who made and destroyed careers during the Golden Era of Hollywood—had known the truth, they *really* would have had something to write about! Max could be challenging, especially emotionally. I am a joyful person today, and I was then. I loved my work, the company of friends, the sunny LA weather, a ride in my convertible, and sharing good times with this very appealing man. But Max tended to be moody, and being provocative was his way of keeping life interesting.

One night, we were in his suite at the Chateau Marmont when he came up with the ultimate test of my feelings for him.

He took my hand, gazed into my eyes, and said, "If you really love me, you'll jump out the window."

I looked at him to see if he was serious, thinking, *We're on the third floor.* Was he insane?

Luckily, my response came to me quickly. I turned to Max and said, "If you love me, *you* jump first, and I will follow."

It was not the answer he expected. I'd outsmarted him. Max looked out the window, then at me, and said, "Maybe another time."

Even though Max liked to come off as a coolheaded bachelor, he was extremely jealous. I was leaving town for a press conference, and my friend, the actor Seymour Cassel, asked if he could borrow my car while I was away. When Max heard that Seymour was driving my car, he called and demanded that he meet him at some remote location on Mulholland Drive to return the car. Seymour thought this sounded strange—maybe even dangerous—so he told his friend John Cassavetes about the meeting in case something happened to him. John had two words of advice: "Don't go!" Seymour kept the car until I came home from my trip, and Max never told me anything about his jealous fit. That was Max—he thrived on drama, and there was more to come.

In the middle of shooting *Flower Drum Song*, I had to fly to Paris for two days to attend the premiere of *The World of Suzie Wong*. When I boarded the plane, I was surprised to see Katharine Hepburn and Mary Pickford, two screen legends, sitting nearby. But I was even more surprised when Katharine Hepburn turned to me and said in her distinctive voice, "Spencer says hello." I thought to myself, how did Spencer Tracy know about my trip to Paris? Max must have told him, and how lovely that Spencer asked Katharine, his partner in a discreet romantic relationship for decades, to give me a message. Meeting these memorable ladies whom I admired in so many wonderful films was a thrill.

In Paris, I checked into the George V Hotel, unpacked, and sent the dress I planned to wear to the premiere to be pressed. A couple of hours later, the hotel manager called and asked if he could come up and see me. He apologized for disturbing me but had terrible news. The woman who ironed my dress burned a hole in it. He was so sorry and quickly assured me the hotel would pay for another.

When I told him I was supposed to wear the dress to the *Suzie Wong* premiere that night, the poor guy turned pale and started shaking his head. He was so distraught that I could read his mind—*movie star, premiere, ruined dress…big trouble ahead!*

I felt terrible for him and was happy to end his misery. I could never decide what to take on a trip, so I was a chronic over-packer. I brought *four* fully packed suitcases to Paris for this two-day sprint, just in case. This time, it turned out well. I told the hotel manager not to worry. I had another dress (maybe two) for the premiere. He looked so relieved and thanked me profusely. I was more concerned about the poor woman who burned my dress—a mistake that might get her fired—and asked him to give her another chance. He promised he would, and I hope he kept his word.

My time in Paris was a blur of photo ops and congratulatory parties; then, I went back to work. *Flower Drum Song* was made so efficiently that we finished shooting several weeks ahead of schedule, which rarely happens. Everyone worked hard on the production because musicals were high-risk investments that could be big winners or even bigger losers at the box office. But many of us also believed that this project, if successful, could be an antidote to the discrimination Asians experienced in Hollywood.

It occurs to me that another form of discrimination was hiding in plain sight, and it affected people who worked on our film every day. Ross Hunter, Hermes Pan, and Irene Sharaff (and, obviously, many others) were gay at a time when a public admission of their sexuality would have instantly ended their careers. They had lived through the Lavender Scare in the 1950s when Joseph McCarthy said that homosexuality was as dangerous a threat to the American way of life as communism. Unlike their Asian American coworkers, who were pinning their hopes on the transformative power of *Flower Drum Song*, they knew the possibility of change or acceptance was not likely, so they led secret lives.

Though Ross had lived happily with designer/producer Jacques Mapes, his long-standing life partner, since the 1940s, he perpetuated the idea that he was a ladies' man. Even in the late 1980s—after Rock Hudson announced that he had AIDS and later died from the disease—Ross, who discovered Hudson and made him a star, insisted to a reporter that "I didn't even know Rock was gay."

Hermes, a devout Roman Catholic, was rumored to have a relationship with dancer Gino Malerba in his later years but was always highly discreet about his personal life. David Patrick Columbia, who collaborated with Hermes on an unpublished memoir in the 1980s, and had great insight into his life, said that "Pan's sexuality was a burden for him"—not a tragic one, he pointed out, but a burden nonetheless.

Irene met her partner, the writer and painter Mai-mai Sze, in the 1930s. They lived and often traveled together but never publicly acknowledged their private relationship. Sze died in 1992, and Irene passed away eleven months later. The two women made a joint bequest to Lucy Cavendish College in England, where their ashes are buried beneath the same rock.

Ross, Hermes, and Irene had every right to keep their private lives to themselves; still, it was wrong that they were forced to do so. I didn't think about it then, but I do now, and I understand that maintaining a public image must have been difficult. I'm sorry they had to live that way, but I admire their resilience.

My first chance to see *Flower Drum Song* was at the Radio City Music Hall premiere in New York in December. I had made two movies in one life-changing year (a big twist of fate for someone who imagined opening a ballet school in Hong Kong), and I had experienced red-carpet excitement at several premieres, but this one exceeded my expectations.

The movie began with a beautiful title sequence created by the Chinese American artist Dong Kingman. Dong was born in California and raised in Hong Kong, then returned to America, where he became a celebrated artist and cultural ambassador. Ross Hunter commissioned him to paint a series of watercolors to tell the story of Mei Li's ocean crossing from China to San Francisco. Accompanied by Rodgers and Hammerstein's overture, the images charted her journey and magically dissolved into the real-life scene of her arrival in Chinatown. This visually stunning opening set the tone for the musical, suggesting that it would transport the audience to a colorful new world.

One of the film's high points was the dream sequence (a staple in a Rodgers and Hammerstein show) dramatizing "Love Look Away," my favorite song in *Flower Drum Song*.

The dance, performed beautifully by Reiko Sato, tells a sad story of unrequited love, a touching subplot in the film and, unfortunately, an ongoing situation in Reiko's life.

Reiko and I were both trained ballerinas who shared a love of dance. We became good friends during the production, and she told me about her relationship with Marlon Brando. When I first came to Hollywood, reporters always asked me how I felt about Marlon, who often had love affairs with "exotic" (meaning Asian) women. Would I, the new girl in town, be his next conquest? While I admired Marlon as an actor, I had no interest in him and said exactly that. Reiko, I learned, was one of the many women who succumbed to Marlon's charms. She was deeply disappointed because what had started as a love affair in the mid-1950s had

94

turned into a friendship. Reiko identified with her character in the film and expressed her feelings about unrequited love in the ballet, making her performance even more powerful.

I was thrilled when the audience at the premiere had the kind of spontaneous reaction that usually only happens in a Broadway theater. They applauded at the close of "I Enjoy Being a Girl" and were equally enthusiastic when the credits came up after the film's romantic finish. We—my castmates who were with me that night—felt appreciated...and *seen*.

While making the film, we saw it as a groundbreaking moment for Asian actors because we finally had our own movie, a main-stream Hollywood production. Benson Fong, who had witnessed (and experienced) the racial barriers that prevented great talents such as Anna Mae Wong from having the success she deserved, told *Variety* that, thanks to *Flower Drum Song*, Hollywood had become more open-minded toward "Oriental" film actors as he described them. He was optimistic that there would be more opportunities for roles in the future.

But as I watched the film at the premiere, I realized *Flower Drum Song* had a cultural, social, and psychological significance extending far beyond employment opportunities in Hollywood because it shattered so many stereotypes. The characters in the film dressed in the latest fashions: The women in the "Sunday" fantasy number could have stepped right out of the pages of *Vogue*. And thanks to Ross's exquisite eye for detail, we lived in beautifully decorated homes—he couldn't rest until he found the perfect carved bed, a valuable antique, for Wang Chi-Yang's bedroom.

Instead of being demonized, marginalized, or portrayed as the "other," our characters were attractive, appealing, affluent, and larger-than-life. We went to nightclubs, drove sports cars, spoke snappy dialogue, and sang! James Shigeta was a handsome heartthrob. Jack Soo was cool enough to be in Frank Sinatra's Rat Pack. And I, or rather, Linda Low, was the girl who had everything—brains, beauty, and all the right moves. *Flower Drum Song* offered the Asian community an opportunity to see idealized versions of themselves: men who were virile and women who were independent and glamorous.

Notably, the minor roles usually assigned to Asians in films—a gardener and a petty thief, for example—were played by Caucasians in *Flower Drum Song*, an ironic twist on Hollywood typecasting. I'm sure Ross did that on purpose.

In Arthur Dong's excellent book, *Hollywood Chinese*, he writes that *Flower Drum Song* "represented an unparalleled and unprecedented milestone for both the film industry and the Asian American community. During the first decades of its release, it was the first time that many Americans were given a picture of Chinatown beyond the exotic tourist facades." This joyful positive representation in a feature film wouldn't be repeated until 2018 when *Crazy Rich Asians* became an international blockbuster.

Dong interviewed several prominent Asian Americans about their reactions to *Flower Drum Song*, and I found their responses (and their criticisms) fascinating. Amy Tan, the author of *The Joy Luck Club*, recalls that she was an impressionable teenager when she saw it and had some reservations about its authenticity. Why, she wondered, was a Japanese woman cast to play a Chinese immigrant? But she recognized the film's impact. "If you were old enough to see it for the first time when it came out, *Flower Drum Song*, I think, influenced every Chinese American kid."

Playwright David Henry Hwang remembered liking the film as a child. However, as he got older and became more politically aware, he questioned the film's portrayal of Chinese Americans and their culture. He was mystified by the musical number "Chop Suey," which celebrated a dish he described as "created to satisfy the white tastes of people who wouldn't feel comfortable eating actual Chinese food." Ultimately, Hwang decided that *Flower Drum Song*, with its "wonderful performances...great music...and amazing dance," was a "guilty pleasure," and, in 2002, with the approval of the Rodgers and Hammerstein Foundation, staged a revival of the musical reimagined for contemporary audiences.

I was touched when actress Ming-Na Wen thanked me for being a role model when she described her reaction to *Flower Drum Song*. "To see someone young and vibrant and sassy who's an Asian American, it just really spoke to me," she said.

I loved *Flower Drum Song* when I saw it at the premiere, and I still love it today. Others loved it, too. After the film came out, whenever I went to a Chinese restaurant, I was lavished with incredible attention and a free meal! Sixty years later, people *still* tell me they remember it well. Times change and new standards of political correctness evolve, but I think the film's accomplishments outweigh any perceived flaws. While a Japanese actor would not play a Chinese character today, in 1961, casting any Asian instead of a Caucasian wearing yellowface represented progress and was a significant victory.

Flower Drum Song should be remembered as a joyous entertainment with the universal message that whatever our race, we're all alike. We cherish our children even when we disagree with them. We fall in love and suffer heartbreak. We make foolish choices and silly mistakes. We laugh, sing, dance, and, most of all, yearn for happily ever after. Moviegoers in 1961 could watch this story and think, maybe for the very first time, *Asians, they're just like us.* I hope the film and its message about our shared humanity continues to inspire people to believe that East *can* meet West and possibly make the world a little better.

CHAPTER 10

The question was, what to do next? Ray was committed to the idea of my becoming the next Audrey Hepburn and truly believed I could play any role, regardless of nationality. "Don't make the mistake of thinking this little girl is only Suzie Wong or Linda Low or even Nancy Kwan," he often said. "Nancy is a girl of many nations, packaged on one body."

Ray demonstrated his open-mindedness when he suggested I star in *The Main Attraction*, a love story set in a European traveling circus. Scripted by John Patrick, who also wrote *The World of Suzie Wong*, the film was about a young circus bareback rider who falls for a handsome drifter with a troubled past. I would play the ingenue, who seemed to be vaguely Italian. And, while I missed out on the opportunity to work with Elvis, I would co-star with *Billboard*'s second most popular male singer, Pat Boone.

Pat's songs, whether romantic ballads or gospel crossovers, were chartbusters. He also starred in a hit television show, and when he made his Elvis-like transition to film in the late fifties, the results were equally successful—*April Love* and *Journey to the Center of the Earth* were big hits. But his recent pictures had gotten a tepid reaction, prompting Pat to think about changing his image. His usual brand was wholesome movies, the kind his daughters could see (Pat famously asked his wife's permission before kissing his leading lady on-screen). But if he wanted to grow as an actor, he'd have to play more dramatic and even edgier roles. "I want to prove to myself that I can be something else on the screen than just Pat Boone," he explained.

Ray proposed that *The Main Attraction* could solve Pat's career dilemma. He'd play Eddie, a morally conflicted roustabout who temporarily loses his way but is saved by the love of an innocent young woman, and he would get to sing and play the guitar. Pat was enthusiastic about Ray's plan to cast him in a more mature role, one that was racier than anything his fans had seen him do before, and he optimistically believed his character's ultimate redemption would justify any adult behavior or sexual content in the film.

Ray planned to shoot at Shepperton Studios in London. He assembled a first-rate British production team, including Daniel Petrie, the director of the critically acclaimed *A Raisin in the Sun*, and cinematographer Geoffrey Unsworth, who photographed *The World of Suzie Wong* (and went on to shoot *Cabaret* and *2001: A Space Odyssey*). I looked forward to reteaming with Geoffrey because he had a great sense of humor. When we made *Suzie Wong*, he teasingly pretended that my youth was a problem and promised to make me look beautiful despite the challenge.

I was also happy about the location—my brother still lived in London, and I felt at home in the city, and Max would be shooting his next film in Europe. Seven Arts Productions, the producing arm of Seven Arts, worked with my manager to set me up in an apartment owned by Peter Sellers, who had starred in the company's controversial hit, *Lolita*. I found it funny that there was a celebrity real estate network for nomadic actors—my apartment in Los Angeles belonged to Rock Hudson.

Ray arranged for Jeff Corey, my acting teacher, to move to London to work with me. Then, it made sense for Pat to take lessons from Jeff, too. Pat's previous films never required him to show a dark side, but this character had to be rebellious, desperate, angry, and even violent. He also had to engage in passionate love scenes that were nothing like the chaste embraces in his previous films. Pat relied on Jeff to refine his technique and help him express these new emotions more authentically. They got along so well that they collaborated on the film's title song.

In the months leading up to the film, I continued my acting lessons and practiced the bareback riding routines I had to perform in the circus scenes. I was comfortable on horseback— I started riding at fourteen when I enrolled in Miss Margaret's Riding Academy while I was studying at Kingsmoor and fell in love with a horse named Nell. Girls and their horses! I groomed Nell, cleaned her stable, and fed her. It was a big responsibility for a teenager, but I never minded the hard work. Nell was a gentle mare who seemed to return my affection.

The one time I had a problem with her, it was entirely my fault. I was on a trail with my friend Lucy, who was older and a more experienced rider. Suddenly, Lucy and her horse, Romeo, galloped ahead. Not wanting to be left behind, I squeezed Nell's flanks with my calves and told her to *go*! Startled, she bucked and sent me flying into the air. I landed on the ground, dazed. Lucy managed to catch up with Nell and brought her to me. I stood up slowly to make sure I didn't feel any pain. Then Lucy asked if I needed help. I shook my head because I understood what I had to do. *Get back on the horse.* I put aside my discomfort and fear, placed my foot in the stirrup, mounted Nell, and rode back to the stable.

It was a good lesson in riding...and in life. I might fall or fail, but I'd get right back on the horse. I would never give up.

I thought of Nell (and that fall) when I started training for the circus. Bareback riding was complicated. I had to learn to stand on the horse's back and leap on and off as it trotted around the ring. Circus performers spend years mastering these moves, but I had to learn them in a few weeks. Years of ballet practice gave me the advantage of strong legs and good balance. Still, there was always the possibility that I could fall, and I did. Even though my harness protected me from serious injury, I was often bruised and uncomfortable.

Max was so concerned about me that he flew to London. There was a little friction between us because Max had given a jaw-dropping answer to columnist Hedda Hopper when she asked when he would propose to me. He said, "Why don't you ask me when I'm going to commit suicide, Hedda?" I knew he resented her impudent question. I felt the same way. But his answer was so outrageous that it was reprinted in other publications, and I was portrayed as *poor Nancy*—waiting for a proposal that was unlikely to happen.

I wasn't waiting, I was working! And I also had doubts about the future of our relationship. Could two busy actors have a viable marriage, especially if we wanted a family? And if he could ask me to jump out a window to prove my love, what might he think of next?

Max arrived in London with a surprise gift—an adorable dachshund. I named him Othello because I was so impressed by

Laurence Olivier's performance at the Old Vic Theater. I wasn't even sure if pets were allowed in my apartment. The building had only three flats, one on each floor, and sound traveled. I could always tell when the people upstairs had guests. I hoped the other tenants couldn't hear Othello's constant barking.

I didn't know much about caring for a dog, but I soon discovered that British people love dogs and are always ready to offer advice. I took Othello everywhere, to the riding school and later to the studio for rehearsals. Sue, my stand-in, was kind enough to watch him while I worked.

On the first day of filming, I decided it would be best to leave Othello in the flat. I gave him food and water, spread newspapers on the kitchen floor, and told him where to do his business. Why did I think he would listen?

When I got home that night, Othello was so excited to see me that he started barking before I opened the door. The kitchen was a mess; he managed to miss the newspaper every time, and most of his "business" was on the floor. Of course, I stepped in it. There were stains on the carpet in the living room and the hallway. Peter Sellers would not be pleased.

I just sat there looking at him—he was too cute to scold. Instead, I called Max in Munich and told him what happened. I asked if he could take care of Othello for me until I finished the film. He was sorry, but the answer was no because he was starting a movie in Rome shortly. I resigned myself to being a single parent with a very demanding four-legged child.

After cleaning the flat, I fell into bed exhausted. The following day, I took Othello to the studio and kept him in my dressing room, hoping he wouldn't bark while the cameras rolled. Sue felt sorry for me and Othello and offered a temporary solution.

She'd take him home, where he could play with Sam, her golden retriever. I was sad but relieved. Then, when I was preparing to leave for location filming, Sue asked if she could keep Othello. Her family had fallen in love with him, and the two dogs were inseparable. I had to think about what was best for Othello and let him go. Sue promised to take good care of him.

I never saw Othello again, but I think about him whenever I open my jewelry drawer. Max gave me a gold and emerald broach shaped like a dachshund, a reminder of my mischievous puppy.

It's a good thing Othello wasn't there the night I came home from work to find Bette Davis and her daughter sitting on my couch. "Oh, hello," she said in her unmistakable voice. They were on their way to Cannes for a presentation of *Whatever Happened to Baby Jane*, another film produced by Seven Arts. Davis told me they had a long layover between flights, so the company parked them in my apartment, where they would be comfortable. Seven Arts must have thought the actors who worked for them were part of one big, happy, thespian family because they never asked my permission. Not that I minded. I admired Bette Davis and couldn't believe she was here in my living room, chatting with me like an old friend.

The Main Attraction had to move to a wintry mountain location because snow was critical to the plot. John Patrick had come up with a novel spin for his modern-day circus story. Usually, characters run away from home to join the circus. In this case, the main characters run away *from* the circus. Pat leaves because he thinks he accidentally killed a man during a brawl, and I bolt after my brother-in-law makes an inappropriate advance. We team up on the road and spend a romantic night at an empty chalet in the mountains, not realizing we're in the path of a deadly avalanche. We fall in love, get rescued at the eleventh hour, and return to the circus for our happy ending when Pat learns the man he thought he killed survived the fight. The movie ends with Pat singing the title song, something his fans would expect. Ray covered all the bases.

Our love scenes at the chalet were considered risqué because—shockingly, in 1962—they involved premarital sex. Or, I should say, the suggestion of premarital sex. It was all very discreet. I'm costumed in a white, chin-to-toe nightgown (with long sleeves) that looks like it was made for a nun, and the scene didn't have an ounce of steam in it. Yet Pat began to worry that anything sexual might offend his fans. Ray reminded him that he wanted a more virile image and promised he would feel differently when he saw the finished film.

Flash forward to later in 1962—seeing the film did not change Pat's mind. He was shocked when *The Main Attraction* failed to get a seal of approval from the Production Code Administration, Hollywood's self-administered censorship division. Then, the Legion of Decency chimed in, classifying the film as "morally objectionable in part for all" and warning that the "glamorization and casual acceptance of premarital sex on the part of the principal characters are particularly dangerous in a film with a special appeal to teenage audiences." Pat agreed with that assessment and was so unhappy that he offered to reshoot the offending scenes. On the other hand, Ray was thrilled about the controversy and anticipated that the promise of sex would boost ticket sales when the film came out.

We were supposed to film in Tuscany, but unfortunately, there was no snow, which is a big problem for a movie with a climactic scene featuring an avalanche. Instead, we went to Kühtai, Austria, and settled in a picturesque resort in the Alps. I was having lunch with a few people from the film at a hotel owned by the Pock family when a young man came over and introduced himself. He was Peter Pock, the owner's polite—and very attractive—son. We chatted, and he told us he was a professional chef and a ski instructor. He also mentioned that he knew everyone at the resort and all the best places to go. If we needed anything, he'd be happy to take care of it. He was so helpful and charming that I invited him to the set to watch the filming.

Peter came the next day, and we visited between takes. Were we flirting? Apparently, because he asked if I'd like to go dancing with him. I was drawn to this appealing young man who was boyish and uncomplicated, like a breath of fresh Alpine air. We spent the evening at a small nightclub in one of the local hotels. The soft lighting was conducive to romance. After that, Peter and I went out almost every night, and while we danced, we seemed to be falling in love.

Why Peter? My career had thrust me into a world where most people I encountered were older than me and focused on their careers. Max was thirty-one, while I was turning twenty-three. Peter was closer to my age and had the same sense of fun and adventure. Whether we were frolicking in the snow or playing chess (Peter was a good chess player, and I always lost to him), we enjoyed each other's company. We didn't care how we spent our time as long as we were together. Best of all, there was no drama—no jealous fits, no existential questions, and no ego. We were just a girl and a boy having a good time.

A surprise call from Max punctured our idyllic bubble. He was in Innsbruck and asked to see me. I had my driver take me to his hotel, about an hour from Kühtai. I suspected our meeting would be awkward—we hadn't seen each other since London, and so much had happened. Max was fresh from his victory at the Academy Awards, where he had won Best Actor for his work in *Judgment at Nuremberg*, a remarkable achievement considering the other nominees were his co-star Spencer Tracy, Paul Newman in *The Hustler*, Charles Boyer in *Fanny*, and Stuart Whitman in *The Mark*. But I doubted he was here to celebrate.

Tonight, the elephant in the room would be Peter. I knew I had to face Max about my change of heart sooner or later, but I was not looking forward to his reaction. He was volatile at times—it would be a bumpy ride.

I told the driver to wait for me when we arrived at the hotel. Max opened the door to his room, and I saw his Oscar displayed on a table. I congratulated him and told him he deserved it—he was terrific in the film. He stared at me for a moment, then asked if it were true that I was having an affair. I nodded, unable to come up with the right words. Finally, I found my voice and told him I was sorry, I had met someone else, and we should stop seeing each other.

In an instant, Max picked up the Oscar and threw it at me. I ducked to avoid it and heard the heavy statue hit the floor with a loud thud. Max stood there, breathing heavily and glaring at me. Afraid of what might happen next, I bolted and ran to the car.

Subsequently, one of the hotel workers told me that Max checked out so quickly that he forgot his Oscar. Eventually, he came back to retrieve it.

I wasn't happy about the way things ended. I never wanted to hurt Max. But I was relieved that our painful breakup was in the past, and now I was free to concentrate on my work and Peter. One of the best things about having a romance at a remote ski resort in Austria was privacy. No reporters. No cameras. No daily reports about how our relationship was—or wasn't—progressing. We could be ourselves, by ourselves, and that sense of intimacy made us feel closer to each other.

The Main Attraction finished shooting, and I returned to London—but I wouldn't be there long because I was scheduled to start shooting my next film—*Tamahine*, in Tahiti. I missed Peter and couldn't figure out how we could maintain a long-distance relationship. Then, he came to visit me. Our feelings for each other were still intense. Love is a powerful emotion. It rules the heart and makes anything seem possible. We were only in our twenties, and we'd known each other for just a few months and came from different backgrounds. Somehow, none of that seemed important. We wanted to be together, and there was one crazy solution. We'd get married!

We planned a simple civil ceremony at the Paddington Registry Office. My assistant took care of all the arrangements, and a fashion designer friend made me a beautiful white lace wedding dress with a fitted bolero jacket. Her seamstresses were Greek and very superstitious, so they sewed good luck charms into the fabric.

I needed all the good luck I could get. I was terrified to tell my father I was getting married. That would be enough of a shock, but marrying someone he never met? I didn't dare call him. I took the coward's way out and asked my brother KK to do it. "I'm not going to do that," he protested, knowing the conversation would not be pleasant. And he didn't think I should get married, either. Finally, he agreed to make the call, but only if I stood at his side when he dropped the bomb. Then, I would have to speak to my father.

Daddy raised all the objections I expected, mainly that I was too young to get married. Of course, I didn't listen. I was rushing into marriage *because* I was too young to know better. I promised we would come to Hong Kong as soon as possible so he could meet his son-in-law.

The civil ceremony, attended by my brother and a few of our friends, was brief. When we left the registry, I was surprised to see reporters crowding outside, their cameras poised. Only our closest friends knew about the wedding, so I had no idea how word got out. We rushed to a small reception at my flat while news of our marriage, accompanied by a photo of the happy couple, made international headlines.

Hollywood reeled from the shock of the Kwan/Schell breakup. A magazine that planned to run a big story about our on-again/off-again romance had to pull that cover at the last minute and scramble to introduce Peter Pock, the mystery groom, to its readers. Gossip columnists immediately chastised Max for dragging his heels. One wrote, "Nancy Kwan's surprise marriage to Peter Pock left Max Schell in the cold. Is he over it?" Another columnist suggested that Max, "no matter how glacial his exterior," was suffering. "The few close to Max believe the Oriental beauty gave him a big jolt right under his ribs on the left side where it hurts." And a third called him "The unhappiest man in Europe...since the girl he loved so long married that Austrian skiing instructor. He thought Nancy would always be there. There's a big moral here."

Max and I never saw each other again, but he called me many years later. He told me he was married and had a daughter. I was happy for him and wished him well.

Peter and I flew to Hong Kong right after the wedding. We celebrated with a party and a traditional wedding ceremony at

Grandfather's church, where my father walked me down the aisle. He seemed to like Peter, but he confided to me that he still had reservations about our future. I wonder if he saw parallels to when he brought Marquita home to meet his family and if he feared our marriage would have the same unhappy outcome. He may have foreseen problems, but with youthful optimism, I envisioned a beautiful future.

CHAPTER 11

Tamahine is an enchanting story about a young, free-spirited Polynesian girl sent to live with her uncle, the proper headmaster of a boys' school in England. The classic fish-out-of-water situation would allow me to develop my comedic skills, something I was eager to do. The locations—London, the English countryside, Paris, and the fantasy island of Bora Bora—made the project even more enticing because I imagined honeymooning with Peter whenever I had a break from filming.

There was one complication I hadn't anticipated. I started feeling a little off—not sick, but not my usual energetic self. When the sight (and smell) of food made me want to run in the other direction, preferably to the nearest restroom, I realized that I was pregnant. We were having a baby! A baby who seemed intent on reminding me of its presence with daily bouts of morning sickness. I was too happy and excited to care about a little nausea—I was healthy, and the production team was very supportive. If I started showing, cinematographer Geoffrey Unsworth (this was our third film together, so we knew each other very well) would hide my bump from the camera. We'd figure it out.

While we were preparing *Tamahine*, an offer for another role came my way. Writer/director Blake Edwards was casting *The*

Pink Panther (starring my landlord, Peter Sellers). Would I be interested in playing Princess Dala?

I had heard that Audrey Hepburn was Blake's first choice but that she couldn't do the film because she was pregnant. Now, *I* had to pass because the start date was in a few months, and I'd be visibly pregnant by then, not a good look for a sexy princess. Blake seemed to think Mother Nature had something against him. "I don't know what's happening with these women," he complained. "They're all pregnant!"

One of the executives at Seven Arts—not Ray—told me I was crazy to let *The Pink Panther* slip away. It would be a big film, and I should be more conscious of my career. "Maybe you could get an abortion," he suggested, pointing out that I could always have another baby. My incredulous response was "What?" Some actresses may have followed that kind of advice, but I wasn't one of them. The conversation was shocking and a flashing red light. This business could be ruthless in ways I'd never imagined.

Tamahine, on the other hand, was a joyful experience, beginning with my reunion with Guy LaRoche in Paris. Fran Stark arranged for him to design my character's post-Tahiti costumes, which were gorgeous. I couldn't wait to show Peter my favorite places in Paris, especially a restaurant I loved. We went there for dinner, but when the waiter served our meal, the smell hit me, and not in a good way. I felt sick, jumped up from the table, and fled to the ladies' room. Peter had to explain to the maître d' that my pregnancy, not the food, sent me running.

Our first location was Wellington College in Berkshire, England, where we filmed the boarding school scenes. I was in very good company if I wanted to learn about comedy. Dennis Price, John Fraser, Coral Browne, Michael Gough, James Fox, and Derek Nimmo were excellent character actors who understood the importance of spontaneity. They taught me that it's a mistake to think *this scene is funny, so I will play it funny.* That rarely works. It's better to react naturally in the moment so the comedy feels real, not canned.

Coral Browne, best known for playing the deliciously vicious Vera Charles in *Auntie Mame,* had a wicked sense of humor, and I loved watching her in action. In one scene, we drove down the Champs-Elysees in a vintage convertible. Coral turned to me and said, "Let's pretend we're royalty and wave to the public." She held up her hand and started waving to the spectators lined up to watch the filming. Feeling like an idiot, I put my hand up and followed suit. Some of the people waved back! She was fearless and always knew how to get a laugh.

By the time we left for Tahiti and Bora Bora, my morning sickness had passed, and I could appreciate the beautiful location. The water was so clear we could see the colorful fish swimming in the lagoon and its surrounding coral reefs. Peter and I toured the island on bicycles, stopping to pick mangoes from the many fruit trees.

At night, we went dancing at the Bora Bora Hotel. The locals showed me a traditional dance characterized by rapid hip-shaking motions. In no time, my hips were going a mile a minute. The next evening, we were having a ball on the dance floor when I noticed there were only four of us left. I asked the waiter what happened. Where did everyone go? He said, "They go to make love." I expected him to laugh and tell me it was a joke, but he just smiled and walked away. Later, I heard there was an accident; one of the romantic Tahitian couples who left the dance floor that night made love under a coconut tree, and a coconut fell on the man's head, knocking him unconscious.

The Tahitians had their way of doing things. We were setting up the scene showing my departure to England. I wore a gray coat, thick stockings, and clunky shoes, and my hair was braided into two fat pigtails. I felt like Little Orphan Annie. About twenty extras, boys and girls from the island, were supposed to line up to say goodbye and kiss me on both cheeks as I walked to the boat.

When the assistant yelled "action," all the extras rushed toward me simultaneously, nearly knocking me over. On the second take, the extras were told to come up to me individually. It went better this time, except one of the boys kissed me on the lips, and another grabbed my breasts. I didn't know how I should react.

The assistant decided it was time for a break. He told the extras to relax for a few minutes, not realizing they would jump in the water. They couldn't be dry in the first shot and wet in the next, so we had to wait for them to dry off before we could resume shooting, an unwelcome delay when time is money.

We wrapped after a very long day, and the extras were told to come get their money. I saw some of them, cash in hand, jump into the ocean for a swim, completely unconcerned when the money floated away. Later, the assistant told me a few extras didn't even bother to get paid. It occurred to me that money was meaningless to them because they had everything they needed and more. Their island home was beautiful and unspoiled. Food—fresh fish and endless varieties of fruit—was abundant.

The Tahitians seemed so relaxed and laissez-faire. Maybe *we* had the wrong approach to life.

I was sad to leave this island paradise, but we had to return to England to finish filming—and in the nick of time. The baby was getting big, and we were running out of ways to disguise the fact that lithe Tamahine was an expectant mother. I wondered what my baby thought about all the traveling and promised him or her there would be more adventures in the future.

Peter and I returned to Austria because we'd decided to have the baby at a hospital in Innsbruck. When the day arrived, March 28, 1963, the baby took hours to come into the world. The delivery was long and painful—sometimes unbearably so. Someone once told me if the birth were painful, it would end in pain, but I tried not to think about that. I passed out during labor, and when I opened my eyes, I thought I had died and gone to heaven. Peter was standing next to my bed in a white gown. I was so confused that I asked him why he was in heaven before me. He assured me we were still here on Earth. Just before I lost consciousness again, I heard him say, "It's a boy!"

Bernhard Pock, or Bernie, as we called our blond, blue-eyed baby, was not just a boy. He was sunshine, pure joy, and the love of my life. When I held him, I thought... *everything has changed.* Before Bernie, my priority was Me, Me, Me. Now, it was the Baby, the Baby, the Baby. I used to be adventurous, even reckless, but motherhood made me cautious. I even drove more carefully. I loved being a mother, *his* mother, which made me feel conflicted about going back to work when he was an infant. Intellectually, I knew that Bernie was too young to be aware of my absence, but I had painful memories of being abandoned by my mother and never wanted my son to experience that feeling.

But I had a contract, so another movie was inevitable. I was a little more enthusiastic about the prospect when Ray Stark showed me an intriguing new script. *The Wild Affair* was a comedy about modern mores in soon-to-be swinging London. I would play Marjorie Lee, a young secretary who lives with her solid and respectable British parents and plans to marry her solid and respectable British boyfriend. As her wedding day approaches, she wonders if she should assert her independence by having one wild affair before she settles down. Her naïve attempt to answer this question has comic consequences.

When Ray told producer Ed Feldman that he was casting me in the lead role, Ed said, "You can't do that; the role is written for an English girl and Nancy's Asian." But Ray had made up his mind and chastised Ed for being so narrow-minded. "The trouble with you, Ed, is that you have to learn to think out of the box," he told him; remarkably, there was no "box" in *The Wild Affair*. Screenwriter/director John Krish could have added a backstory to the script explaining that my character was Eurasian, the daughter of an English father and a Chinese mother. Instead, he left it exactly how it was, believing the audience would accept me as Marjorie. Race wasn't an issue.

Krish, who went on to make award-winning documentaries about British life, wanted his film to capture London's exciting *now*: 1963, the beginning of the city's reign as the youthquake capital of the world. The Swinging Sixties wouldn't be in full bloom until a few years later, but at this pivotal time, young Brits were discovering that "mod" meant shorter skirts, louder music, and looser morals, an intoxicating alternative to a life of postwar "keep calm and carry on." Marjorie's dilemma about whether to embrace her parents' values or be more adventurous was the story of her generation.

I knew London well, and I saw—and heard—signs of change everywhere. The music! The Beatles had just released their first album, *Please Please Me*. I listened to another new group, the Rolling Stones, at one of their early concerts in a small and smokey West End club. Their sound was exciting, but the room was such a crush of throbbing bass and thrashing bodies that I fainted and had to be taken outside for a reviving gulp of fresh air.

If you knew your way around the King's Row (and I did), the shopping was catnip to anyone who wanted to look more tomorrow than today. Bazaar was *the* store, and its high priestess was the young designer Mary Quant, who stocked it with fitted ribbed sweaters, patterned tights, glossy boots, and dresses and skirts that seemed to get shorter by the minute—a look I loved.

The movie business was changing, too. Rising stars included Julie Christie and an exciting new generation of leading men. Talented (and very handsome) Albert Finney, Terence Stamp, and Michael Caine wore their working-class roots proudly, and their rough edges heightened their appeal. Filmmakers were breaking away from old formulas and searching for new stories and new ways to tell them.

One day, I was at lunch with my actor friends John Derek and Ursula Andress. Ursula entertained us with a description of her new project—a "B" movie, she said—with some guy named Sean Connery playing a character called Bond, James Bond. Ursula had been cast as Honey Ryder, Bond's love interest, and in her first scene, she had to walk out of the ocean dressed (or undressed) in an eye-popping bikini—no problem for Ursula because she was gorgeous.

But a "B" movie??? Far from it. *Dr. No* was the first spy film to be sexy, funny, action-packed, and a blockbuster. James Bond created a new genre, launching legions of 007-styled imitators and a sixty-year-old (and still counting) franchise. Ursula's bikini became such a pop culture icon that, in 2001, it sold at auction to Planet Hollywood for $61,500.

The Wild Affair broke new ground in its own way by being the first film to embrace the revolutionary mod look. Mary Quant designed my costumes, but it wasn't enough for my clothes to reflect the revolutionary spirit of the time; my hair had to make a statement, too. John Krish believed only one person could be entrusted with my waist-length locks: Vidal Sassoon, the daring young hairdresser who created the short, geometric cuts framing the faces of Quant's models.

I had refused when Ross Hunter asked me to cut my hair for *Flower Drum Song*. Why was I willing to do it now? Maybe I was a more mature actress who understood that a physical transformation could help me inhabit the role of Marjorie Lee. Or maybe I liked the idea of a modern new look to go with my new life as a wife and mother. Whatever the reason, I agreed to surrender my schoolgirl mane to Vidal's scissors.

John arranged for us (me, a friend, and the entire Seven Arts production team) to meet Vidal at his salon on New Bond Street. He was a charming man, and even though he was conservatively dressed in a buttoned-up shirt and a tie, he struck me as more of an artist than a hairdresser. He asked me how I felt about cutting my hair. I assured him I was okay with it, but I must have been nervous because I made an unusual request. Would he mind if I played chess while he worked so I wouldn't have to look in the mirror? With his consent, my friend set up a small table, unpacked a miniature chess set, and we started the game.

My hair was over four feet long and thick, so it took time for Vidal to determine the architecture of the cut. He believed hair was an art form, and like Marcel Breuer and Mies van der Rohe, the architects who inspired him, he tried to create new forms and shapes. He studied my bone structure, turning my chin this way and that, then said, "We could do almost anything with Nancy." Out came the scissors, which were like extensions of his hands, and he began cutting. When Vidal cut, he moved his whole body. I, on the other hand, sat like a statue, trying not to react as I felt the unaccustomed sensation of air on my neck. "She was the coolest I've ever seen anybody," Vidal marveled in his autobiography. "She didn't make a movement."

My entourage watched attentively, calculating the outcome as my hair piled on the floor. What if John Krish's daring idea was a big mistake?

After pulling, snipping, and testing for movement, Vidal finally found the look he wanted. Short in the back, graduating to more length on the sides, a modern bob that was angular and sculptural. When he finished, he knew that something extraordinary had happened. "Nancy Kwan had the perfect head of hair for what I had been working towards for so long. She was a gift," he wrote later. "I hadn't planned it, but I was beginning to realize that this was—for me, at least—a seminal moment."

Vidal immediately called Terence Donovan, an irreverent young photographer who, along with David Bailey (the inspiration for the film *Blow-Up*) and Brian Duffy, captured the essence of the London scene with his camera. "I think I've got something!" Vidal told him, describing my radical haircut. His excitement was contagious. Donovan arranged to photograph me that very night, and Vidal gave a heads-up to the art direc-tor of *British Vogue*, who insisted on seeing the proofs the next morning.

Donovan was known for breaking rules and pushing limits. He placed his beautifully dressed fashion models in gritty urban landscapes (one dangling precipitously from a parachute). He cheekily fulfilled every man's dream by posing Julie Christie in bed, peeking from behind a sheet. But he photographed me as if I were a work of art, a classical sculpture of arm, shoulder, neck, and gleaming hair. A Modigliani profile rendered in light and shadow. Somehow, the arresting image was both timely and timeless. As Vidal said, "It had the Donovan magic written all over it."

Mission accomplished; we ended the evening at a Chinese restaurant.

Vogue's art director was so enthusiastic about the photograph that he rushed to include it in the very next issue. It was the snip heard around the world. The portrait, which soon became a beauty icon, ran in *Vogue* and every other international pub-lication. Like my cheongsam, the "Nancy Kwan Cut" was the must-have look for stylish women everywhere, demonstrating that beauty was a universal concept and imitation was the highest form of acceptance.

Vidal was thrilled with the response to his creation. Fashion editors believed he was a visionary who could shape (literally) the future of hair. They were right. He became the most famous hair-stylist in the world and built a global "If you don't look good, we don't look good" empire of salons, beauty schools, and haircare products.

I loved the look of my new hairstyle and thought it was perfect for *The Wild Affair*. Later, I discovered that it took a lot of work to maintain a work of art. The style was *so* sculptural that if one hair grew too long, it destroyed the whole line. My hairdresser in America, who Vidal had trained, had to go back to London to master the secrets of this challenging cut. Eventually, I had to let it grow out, but Terence Donavan's extraordinary photograph made it immortal.

Peter and Bernie had accompanied me to London so I could spend time with them before we started filming. We introduced the baby to my brother KK, my sister Betty, a student at the University of London, and my Aunty Renee, who was visiting from Hong Kong. I invited Vidal to a family dinner at a Chinese restaurant known for its dim sum. Family reunions and good times with friends ended when production started on *The Wild Affair*, and inevitably, I had to send Peter and Bernie back to Kühtai.

The film had a solid cast of British actors. My co-star, Terry-Thomas, was a national treasure. He created the BBC's first comedy series, which ran for five seasons, and frequently starred in riotous comedies with Peter Sellers. His characters often represented the British posh establishment in its funniest and most satirical form. It was impossible *not* to laugh at the sight of the large gap between his front teeth. Terry served a similar comic purpose in *The Wild Affair*, where he played a bewildered middle-aged man who was clueless about the imminent fall of the British Empire.

The shoot was pleasant although coming home to an empty apartment made me realize how much I missed my little family. I was so lonely that I considered asking Peter to bring Bernie back to London, but that would have been selfish. I left for work early in the morning and finished late at night, so I wouldn't have much time to spend with the baby. I knew he was better off with Peter in Austria.

Then, I was troubled by disturbing rumors I heard on set; some people objected to my playing an English girl and thought I should stick to Asian roles instead of robbing British actresses of opportunities meant for them. Really? What about all the Asian roles Caucasians played throughout the entire history of movie-making? I thought we had moved beyond these stereotypes and expected my peers to be more open-minded. I was disappointed that we seemed to be going backward, but I blocked out all the negative thoughts and concentrated on my work.

Which brings me to another point. I approached every film optimistically and always tried to do a good job. That's all you can do. So many elements must come together for a film to succeed, most of which are beyond control. A project might have a great director and a terrific script, but somehow, something goes wrong, and it just doesn't come out as envisioned.

That's what happened with *The Wild Affair*. We made it in 1963, before *Darling, A Hard Day's Night, The Knack*, and other films that portrayed the exciting youth-driven sensibility in London. But instead of being rushed into theaters so it could be a revelatory first, the film was trapped in a distribution bottle-neck and shelved until 1965, a delay that sealed its fate.

Timing is everything. The ideas that had been so cutting edge—especially the au courant costumes and hair—were passé two years later, an echo of the recent past instead of a harbinger of the future. Consequently, the film was largely dismissed.

The bright note for me was when a critic wrote, "You never once bat an eye" at the sight of Nancy Kwan playing a typical

English girl. He said he found me so convincing in the role that he suspended any considerations of race or nationality. That was my goal—to be perceived as an actor and judged for my performance, not my appearance or heritage. To me, that was *real* success.

CHAPTER 12

M y reunion with Bernie was a little bittersweet because I knew it would be brief. The reality of being a working actress was that I had no control over my schedule. My next film, *Honeymoon Hotel*, called for me to start shooting just a few weeks after I finished *The Wild Affair*, and Peter wouldn't be able to join me because he was enrolled in a hotelier course to prepare him for running his parents' hotel. Maybe I was naïve to think I could handle motherhood, marriage, and a career, but I wanted to believe it was possible to do it all.

Honeymoon Hotel is a romantic comedy about the misadventures of two amorous bachelors who unwittingly check into a resort for newlyweds. My co-stars Robert Goulet and Robert Morse were fresh from Broadway, where Goulet had created the showstopping role of Lancelot in Lerner and Loewe's *Camelot*, and Robert Morse had won a Tony Award for his hilarious portrayal of a devious corporate climber in *How to Succeed in Business Without Really Trying*. I was cast as the hotel's social director, the only single woman at the resort, and a whip-smart transplanted New Yorker who is always two steps ahead of the would-be Casanovas who mistake her for an easy conquest.

Sixties sex comedies, as they're called now, featured 1963's idea of the modern woman. Unlike their predecessors, these women had careers, opinions, and incredibly chic wardrobes, *and* they out-smarted men at the mating game. Schooled by Helen Gurley Brown in her bestselling book *Sex and the Single Girl*, this plucky sister-hood rewrote the rules of seduction. Kim Novak turned the tables on James Garner in *Boy's Night Out*. Jane Fonda tamed perennial bachelor Rod Taylor in *Sunday in New York*. *Honeymoon Hotel* fol-lowed the same formula, showing that a clever woman (me) could reform an inveterate playboy (Robert Goulet). The process was all in good fun and almost always involved sexual innuendo, mistaken identity, a lecherous boss, and a bikini or a negligee.

Every studio churned out these crowd-pleasing farces, but MGM took an unusual approach by casting me as their film's lead because the benign romance at the story's center then became interracial, a controversial idea as recently as 1959. (Remember the tagline describing James Shigeta in *The Crimson Kimono*? "Yes, this is a beautiful American girl in the arms of a Japanese boy!") Was the studio's decision a sign of progress, or an acknowledgment of my box office value? Either way, I thought playing a role that wasn't written for an Asian but for a *person* was the right choice. The studio made the project more enticing by giving my character a jazzy dance number. I missed dancing and was eager to get back to it.

So off I went to Hollywood to make the film. Everything I'd heard about the two "Bobs" suggested they'd be congenial co-stars, but I never dreamed they'd be *so* funny, even funnier than the farcical characters they played. Robert Goulet was a charmer, always lightheartedly flirting with the ladies, and Rob-ert Morse was quick-witted and had an endless supply of jokes. It was a good thing the film was a comedy because I couldn't stay serious for a minute when they were around.

The laughter stopped on November 22 when an assistant interrupted a scene to tell us that President John F. Kennedy had been assassinated. We reacted with shock and disbelief, then grief and crying. We were sent home—there would be no filming until further notice—and I raced to my apartment to turn on the news. For the next four days, I sat in front of the television, mesmerized by the uninterrupted coverage of the assassination and the funeral. The entire country was in mourning, and the last thing on anyone's mind was comedy, so I wondered how we could finish the movie.

Nevertheless, we went back to work, the film wrapped, and I was able to return to my family in Austria. I had one thought: Bernie! As soon as I got home, I raced to his playpen and bent down to pick him up. He looked up at me quizzically, then immediately burst out crying. My son didn't recognize me.

I was devastated. There were more separations ahead—my next film started production in just a few weeks—so I had to come up with a better solution than being an absentee mother.

When Bernie was born, my father suggested I hire Ah Yee, the amah who had been with our family for many years. I didn't do it then but was ready to do it now. I grew up with amahs and knew they provided a special kind of childcare. They had a fascinating history. Traditional amahs belonged to a sisterhood that originated in the silk industry, one of China's most profitable exports. These women were hired to raise the silkworms and spin the silk. Their financial independence enabled them to reject arranged marriages and make choices about how they wanted to live their lives. Amahs came to be known as women who lived apart from men, usually sworn spinsters or widows. They banded together to find jobs in the silk factories and, almost like a union, set the wages and terms of their employment. The amahs benefited from their bond, giving each other emotional and even financial support, especially in old age. When an amah retired, she could move into a home for amahs.

During the Depression in the 1930s, the demand for silk and other luxuries plummeted, factories closed, and the amahs transitioned to jobs as domestic workers. They were easy to identify when they came to Hong Kong because they never cut their hair and wore it in a single long braid. The amahs developed a reputation for their dedication to the children in their care. Ah Yee brought up my youngest brother, Teddy, and she was also a great cook. She was the solution I needed: She and Bernie would come with me whenever I traveled. The one problem, which wasn't a problem at all from my point of view, was that she didn't speak English, not one word, which meant that Bernie would have to learn Chinese.

Soon after Ah Yee's arrival, the three of us headed for Los Angeles to film *Fate Is the Hunter*. I would be able to see my baby every day and know that he was in good hands while I was at work. How did Peter feel about this arrangement? We saw each other so infrequently that we rarely had time for serious conversations. I'd finish a film and come home for a few days—a few weeks at the most—then I'd leave to start another film or do publicity for one that was coming out. I felt guilty every single time and knew we were drifting apart. But what could I do? If I gave up my career, I would be *very* unhappy. I went full ostrich and took the easy way out by avoiding the subject although I knew we'd have to talk about it sooner or later.

In *Fate Is the Hunter*, a suspense thriller about a man's desperate attempt to solve the mystery of a tragic plane crash, I played a brainy young oceanographer who helps with the case. My co-star, Glenn Ford, reminded me of Bill Holden, his lifelong friend. These skilled actors, veterans of the Golden Age of Hollywood, had been on-screen for decades. Glenn starred in films as diverse as *Gilda*, with Rita Hayworth (one of the first examples of film noir), *The Teahouse of the August Moon*, the comedy *3:10 to Yuma*, and *The Courtship of Eddie's Father*. Contemporary audiences may remember him as Clark Kent's adoptive father in the top-grossing reboot of the *Superman* franchise, starring Christopher Reeve.

Glenn and Bill taught me that confidence is the key to creating an authentic character. Interestingly, they never improvised, which they would have considered a sign of indecisiveness or insecurity. They believed in themselves and their choices, and once they determined how to approach a character they acted with authority.

I studied with Jeff Corey, Uta Hagen, and at the Actor's Studio and understood that acting teachers offered valuable lessons about technique. But the best classroom has always been the set. Watching other actors at work is a real learning process. The good actors, like Bill and Glenn, showed me how to be better, and the bad ones showed me what *not* to do. Every film, the successes and the failures, helped me improve. I even had the opportunity to learn how to act in a silent film, something that rarely happened in the 1960s.

The Magic Stone, my first—and last—silent film, was my most unusual acting experience. There is a legend in Hong Kong about the Amah Rock, a stone formation that sits atop a hill in the Sha Tin District of the city. The rock looks like a woman carrying a baby on her back. According to the story, that woman, Ling

Two years old and on the beach in Hong Kong, 1941. *Personal Collection*

My mother, Marquita Scott, when she was twenty years old. *Personal Collection*

Me, Aunty Nan, my father, Kwan Wing Hong, my sister Betty, and my grandfather, Kwan Chee Woh, 1946. *Personal Collection*

Ballet with my dancing teacher, Miss Babs Reynolds. I was ten years old, 1949. *Personal Collection*

A daring poster in 1960 for *The World of Suzie Wong* that showed me in an embrace with Bill Holden. © *Paramount Pictures. All Rights Reserved.*

WILLIAM **HOLDEN**

in Ray Stark's

THE WORLD OF **SUZIE WONG**

co-starring **NANCY KWAN** as SUZIE WONG

TECHNICOLOR®

ALSO CO-STARRING
SYLVIA SYMS · MICHAEL WILDING · JOHN PATRICK · RICHARD QUI

TO LET
閣 酒 茗
BAR

One of many happy moments with Bill Holden, a generous actor and a true friend, 1960. © *Paramount Pictures. All Rights Reserved.*

Bill, who played an artist, painting my portrait in *The World of Suzie Wong*, 1960. © *Paramount Pictures. All Rights Reserved.*

Posing for pictures with Fran and Ray Stark at the party they hosted to introduce me to Hollywood, 1960. *Photographer unknown, Personal Collection*

With Kirk Douglas at the star-studded Stark party, 1960. *Photographer unknown, Personal Collection*

Flower Drum Song, 1961. Flower Drum Song *photos courtesy of the Rodgers and Hammerstein Foundation*

Behind the camera during the filming of *Flower Drum Song*'s "I Enjoy Being a Girl," 1961. Flower Drum Song *photos courtesy of the Rodgers and Hammerstein Foundation*

Filming "Fan Tan Fannie," 1961. Flower Drum Song *photos courtesy of the Rodgers and Hammerstein Foundation*

Cary Grant was always the best-looking person in the photograph! On the set of *Flower Drum Song*, 1961. Flower Drum Song *photos courtesy of the Rodgers and Hammerstein Foundation*

Posing with Jack Soo, Miyoshi Umeki, and James Shigeta in a publicity shot for *Flower Drum Song*, 1961. Flower Drum Song *photos courtesy of the Rodgers and Hammerstein Foundation*

The "Grant Avenue" musical number featured two thousand extras and a marching band, 1961. Flower Drum Song *photos courtesy of the Rodgers and Hammerstein Foundation*

With Maximillian Schell, an extraordinary actor, 1961. Flower Drum Song *photos courtesy of the Rodgers and Hammerstein Foundation*

Peter Pock and I at our wedding in Hong Kong, 1962. *Personal Collection*

The "Kwan Cut," the famous hairstyle created by Vidal Sassoon and immortalized by Terrence Donavan in his celebrated photograph, 1963. *Photograph Terence Donovan © Terence Donovan Archive/Camera Press*

Bernhard Pock, the love of my life, 1963. *Personal Collection*

Five-year-old Bernie, my best friend and favorite companion, 1968. *Personal Collection*

David Giler, my
second husband,
1970. *Personal
Collection*

Growing up together
in Hong Kong, 1972.
Personal Collection

Sharon Tate and I
practice our Kung
Fu moves with Bruce
Lee while filming *The
Wrecking Crew*, 1968.
*Courtesy of Columbia
Pictures*

Standing on the Great
Wall of China during
my visit to the country
in 1972. *Personal
Collection*

A meeting with
Bruce Lee and
Raymond Chow,
1972. *Courtesy of
David Tadman*

Finding happiness with
Norbert Meisel, 1977.
Personal Collection

Mother and son, 1980. *Personal Collection*

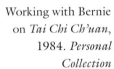

Working with Bernie on *Tai Chi Ch'uan*, 1984. *Personal Collection*

President Bush's Proclamation establishing May as Asian/Pacific American Heritage Month, and the pen he handed to me after he signed it, 1990. *Personal Collection*

President George Bush during the Asian Pacific American Heritage Week ceremony at the White House. Among the Asian Americans honored are from left to right: Dr. Taylor Wang, 1st Asian American Astronaut—payload specialist for May 1985 Skylab I Mission; Virginia Cha, Miss Maryland 1989; I. M. Pei, Architect; Sammy Lee, Olympic gold medalist; Nancy Kwan, actress; Dr. T.D. Lee, Nobel Prize Winner for Physics. *Photo by Jim Davison*

The poster for Bernie's movie, *The Biker Poet*, which was also known as *Rebellious*, 1995. *Personal Collection*

A transformative moment
at Angor Wat, 2011.
Personal Collection

With my brother
KK, his wife,
Moyra, and
Norbert. *Personal
Collection*

A joyous experience
raising funds for
the children in Siem
Reap, 2013. *Personal
Collection*

With Kevin Kwan, 2016.
Personal Collection

Yuen, was the faithful wife of a fisherman. She stood on the hill with her child whenever he went away, watching for his ship. One day, he failed to return because he drowned in a shipwreck. But Ling Yuen continued her sad vigil until the Goddess of the Sea took pity on her and turned her to stone. Her figure, eternally looking out at sea, is a symbol of loyalty and fidelity.

The legend of the Amah Rock has been the subject of many classical poems and is a popular tourist attraction today. At one point, the Hong Kong Film Unit, a government office dedicated to making films about Hong Kong, produced a twenty-four-minute drama about the story and invited me to play the role of Ling Yuen. I had to tell the story and communicate my character's emotions through a naturalistic form of pantomime, which was challenging. In one scene, I had to tell my "husband" I was pregnant with just a whisper in his ear, a shy smile, and a downward glance. It was so interesting to act using carefully chosen facial expressions and gestures instead of dialogue, and I developed a new appreciation for the performances of silent screen stars.

This experience, combined with the wide variety of films I'd done in the past six years, made me a more mature actress, just as motherhood had helped me to become a more responsible adult. But my equilibrium was somewhat shaken by a surprise communication from my mother. After years of silence, she contacted me with an unexpected invitation: Would I like to visit her in Ibiza, where she lived with Pepe, her second husband? I didn't need a mother—that time had passed—but I wondered if we could connect even if our bond wasn't maternal. I accepted her invitation and told my father about my plan to visit her. If he disapproved, he knew better than to try to talk me out of going. I was a grown woman, and I had made up my mind.

I went to Ibiza with no expectations. At worst, the trip would be a vacation in a beautiful place. 1965 Ibiza was still a haven for artists, although later in the 1960s, it would become a destination for jet-setters. Pepe owned a restaurant overlooking the Mediterranean, where we spent hours drinking wine and enjoying the island's rustic beauty. I deliberately didn't broach any difficult subjects when my mother and I were together. I didn't want to hurt her by asking why she left us or why she stayed away for so many years. The past was the past, and I was looking for a way forward.

I found it when I realized that my mother was best cast in the role of friend. She was fun and easy to talk to, and we discussed neutral subjects as we cautiously got to know each other. She loved hearing about my experiences working on films. On one occasion, my stories prompted her to steer the conversation in a more personal direction. She told me that she had always wanted to be an actress but never had a chance to pursue her dream after she married my father. They moved to Hong Kong, she got pregnant, then war broke out. She was unhappy with her new life, and leaving her family was her desperate attempt to revive her lost dream. Although she never accomplished that for herself, she said that when *I* became a successful actress, I fulfilled everything she ever wanted.

I appreciated her honesty but felt conflicting emotions as I listened to her story: sympathy for the misguided young woman whose impulsive choices derailed her life and resentment because her motivations had been so selfish. When I thought about her words, I understood she was trying to tell me I had turned out fine without her. Better than fine because I achieved what she could never do, and her dream lived on in me. Ibiza marked a turning point for us because I could accept my mother for who she was instead of who she should have been. Moving forward, we maintained a warm relationship.

1965 promised to be my busiest year. Seven Arts announced that I would star in three films back-to-back: *No Strings*, *The Deep Freeze Girls*, and *The Fifth Coin*. I had mixed feelings about *No Strings* because Ray Stark stirred up quite a controversy when he paid $2 million for the rights to Richard Rodgers' musical and announced that I would play the lead. *No Strings* is a bittersweet romance about a fashion model and a struggling expatriate writer who have a love affair in Paris. The show was considered groundbreaking at the time because the relationship at its center was interracial; the model was black and the writer white. Acknowledging that the world beyond their idyllic Paris garret would not accept them as a couple, the two lovers separate at the end of the show.

The role was created for Diahann Carroll, whose critically acclaimed performance won her the Tony Award for Best Actress in a Musical in 1962. When Diahann heard Ray's casting announcement, she issued a blistering response, publicly accusing him of "running away from the color issue" because he was "afraid of the reaction in four or five Southern States."

Ray dismissed the idea, explaining that he had a completely different vision for the project. "This isn't going to be a race problem picture the way we're going to do it," he explained. "The picture's going to be a light, happy entertainment"—a Hollywood musical about star-crossed lovers in Paris.

He also defended his reasons for casting me in the role. "We have Nancy Kwan under contract," he said, "and we're always looking for a part to build her up. This is a $3-million to $4-million picture—we had to have a name." He may have thought casting an Asian in the role maintained the film's interracial dynamic.

I understood both points of view. Diahann was concerned about preserving the intention and integrity of the musical. Ray, a businessman, wanted to protect his sizable investment by making the project more mainstream. And here I was, caught in the crossfire. If I turned down a Seven Arts film, I would be suspended without salary. I learned that the hard way when I refused to play an Asian character who spoke pidgin English because I didn't want to perpetuate that terrible stereotype. My resistance had consequences. I was suspended without salary until I agreed to do the next film Seven Arts proposed, and the work interruption extended my contract. So, no, I didn't turn down *No Strings*, but I was not unhappy when the project became so mired in controversy that Ray never made the film.

The second film on my schedule was *The Deep Freeze Girls*, based on a book by Eva Defago. It was described as "the scandalous novel of an exclusive school for girls too young to marry— and too anxious to wait," and I had a feeling the producers would turn it into another "sixties sex comedy." My co-star was Sue Lyon, also a Seven Arts contract player, who was a scandalous sensation in *Lolita* and had just played the teenage temptress in Ray Stark's *The Night of the Iguana*.

The Fifth Coin was the most promising film because the script had been assigned to a very young Francis Ford Coppola. Ray had a keen instinct for emerging talent. Francis was a film student when they met, and Ray was so impressed that he hired him to develop screenplays for Seven Arts. We'd see each other at Ray's parties, where the guests' median age was so old that we felt we should be seated at the children's table.

The concept of *The Fifth Coin*, later called *Kowloon*, was to update the classic film *Casablanca* and set it in Hong Kong. Tony Curtis signed on to play the male lead. *This is the film I've been waiting for*, I thought, the opportunity to play a strong, dramatic role in a story about love and sacrifice.

The future was bright, but first, I had to go to Hawaii to shoot the Disney family comedy, *Lt. Robin Crusoe U.S.N.* Loosely based on the Daniel Defoe novel *The Life and Adventures of Robinson Crusoe*, the film featured Dick Van Dyke as a navy pilot who becomes a castaway on a tropical island. I was "Wednesday," a native princess whose father (played by Akim Tamiroff) banished her to the island because she refused to marry the suitor he selected. I grew up watching Disney movies—a double feature every Saturday—so the idea of being a Disney princess was very appealing, and I was curious to see how the magic was made.

The studio took this project very seriously because Walt Disney himself had come up with the concept of turning Defoe's classic into a contemporary comedy. For example, I had one costume for the entire film. Production had to choose between a red sarong with a flower print and a white sarong with a flower print, which didn't sound complicated. Yet, hours, if not days, were spent determining which was better. They decided the only way to be absolutely certain was to see how the two sarongs looked on film, so I had to do a screen test wearing each one. After much deliberation, the producers picked red.

Every frame of *Lt. Robin Crusoe* was storyboarded, the same process Disney used for their animated films. When I reported for work, I could look at the storyboard and know precisely how many shots I had that day—maybe two medium shots, one close-up, and a long shot—and that's what we'd shoot. One day, director Byron Paul told me to turn my head and gaze out at the ocean. I looked, but we were on a set, and all I could see was film equipment scattered all over the floor. "Don't worry," Byron said. "When you see the film, it will be the ocean. We call it Disney magic."

Dick Van Dyke was naturally funny, and he handled his body so well that he seemed like a trained dancer, which he wasn't. But the most colorful member of our cast was a chimpanzee named Dinky, who played Robin Crusoe's companion. Every time I walked by Dinky's cage, he reached out with his long arms to pat me on my butt. When I smacked his hand away, he gleefully jumped up and down, proud he had gotten away with it. Dinky started his day by sharing a cigarette and coffee with Dick. I'm not sure he was a chimpanzee!

When I finished the film, it was time to think seriously about my career and where it was going. *The Deep Freeze Girls* evaporated, never to be made, which probably wasn't a tragedy because I barely remember it. Then, the Francis Ford Coppola project fell apart, a disappointment. Seven Arts pivoted and plugged me (and Tony Curtis) into another production, a *very* slight comedy called *Arrivederci, Baby!* For some reason, comedies about men trying to murder their wives were popular that year, and *Arrivederci, Baby!* was the same kind of lame bedroom farce. My part was more of a cameo than a leading role, and the only thing I liked about the film was my character's name—"Baby."

To be honest, I was looking forward to the end of my contract with Seven Arts. The perks were easy to love. I had a steady salary and support teams to manage travel, housing, and whatever else came up, especially when I worked on a film. Ostensibly, and this is important, Ray Stark was in my corner, masterminding my career. But Ray had come a long way since our fortuitous meeting in 1959, and so had his company.

Seven Arts, the little engine that *could* in its early days, had expanded into a multilayered production and distribution dynamo. In addition to producing and packaging films, Ray and his partner, Eliot Hyman, set up distribution deals with domestic and international film companies, bought studio libraries and licensed them to television, and invested in real estate. Among their assets were contract players, and the goal was to get a return on their investment in these "properties." Consequently, all decisions about the films I would make were essentially financial. It was better to cast me in *any* movie than to pay my salary while I didn't work, which is how I ended up in *Arrivederci, Baby!* Ed Feldman, who worked with Ray Stark for many years, called the arrangement "indentured servitude." Seven Arts also had the option of loaning me out to other companies for a profit, a profit they pocketed, so the quality of a prospective production wasn't a real consideration: it was more important to keep me working.

I was tired of playing in comedies. I wanted a role I could sink my teeth in—a solid drama or mystery, or a stage musical with dancing. Most of all, I wanted to work with good directors. I was drawn to the filmmakers working outside of the studio system, mavericks like John Cassavetes, who were redefining American cinema in their own backyard.

I met John and his wife, Gena Rowlands, through my friend, Seymour Cassel. John was a talented actor who worked constantly in episodic television during the 1950s and then made a big splash with his role as the villainous husband in Roman Polanski's *Rosemary's Baby.* Acting paid the bills, but John's real passion was directing, and he set off on that path by becoming one of America's first auteurs. He did it all. He wrote screenplays that were provocative studies of modern life, called upon his accomplished friends, including Seymour, to serve as cast and crew, and made small and intensely personal low-budget films that were the antithesis of Hollywood productions.

They were characterized by realistic dialogue, naturalistic (and often unforgiving) lighting, grainy images shot in 16-millimeter, erratic camera movement, and extreme close-ups that saw into the very souls of his actors, John's home-made films were bold, challenging, and exciting because they blurred the lines between art and life.

Shadows, John's directorial debut in 1958, caught the attention of Paramount, prompting the studio to offer him a two-picture deal. His first film was *Too Late Blues,* a moody study of a jazz musician played by Bobby Darin.

Important producers regularly borrowed prints of upcoming movies from the studios and showed them to their friends in their private screening rooms. One night, Ray, who had a relationship with Paramount, invited me to his home to see *Too Late Blues.*

Ray's tented garden parties, like the one he hosted for me, were Hollywood spectacles, but his house was the epitome of quiet, old-money elegance, tastefully decorated with chintz, dark wood, and a stunning array of art. A very private man, Ray frequently invoked the colorful adage, "high profile, broken nose," and was reluctant to talk about himself. He rarely gave interviews, and when asked about his art, he dismissed the notion that he was a collector by saying, "We merely have a lot of things we want to live with."

The "things" the Starks "lived with" were more likely to be found in a museum than in a private residence. Marc Chagall's *L'Esprit de Roses* hung over the fireplace. On another wall, Claude Monet's *Le Bassin aux Nymphéas*, from the original Water Lilies series. In the dining room, Picasso's *Carafe and Tomato Plant*. In the library/screening room, Picasso's *Jacqueline and Boy Eating a Watermelon*. Concealing the projection booth, an important Utrillo. Tucked away in the bedroom, Rene Magritte's *La Forêt Joyeuse*. There were also impressive works of sculpture, including Aristide Maillol's bronze statue, *Baigneuse*, which stood by the front door.

My God, I thought as I walked past this display of works by my favorite artists. *They live with these treasures every day?*

The friends who attended Ray's screenings were as venerable as the masterpieces on his walls—the great directors, John Huston, Vincente Minnelli, Billy Wilder, and the biggest stars. I usually sat in the back with the other "kids," Ray's protégés from the new generation, and the night we watched *Too Late Blues*, we were excited by Cassavetes's irreverent filmmaking. But the Old Hollywood denizens sitting in the front? Not so much. They didn't know what to make of the pore-revealing close-ups, the now-you hear-it, now-you-don't dialogue, and the edgy, realistic story. They were very vocal about their objections. Where was the glamour? "You can see the sweat," one complained. "The studio will never accept this," predicted another.

They were right about that. Paramount was baffled by the film and canceled John's multipicture deal. I was happy he wasn't in the room to hear their damning comments although John had no illusions about the uphill battle he faced in Hollywood. "One thing I learned about studios: you can't please them and yourself at the same time," he told the *New York Times*. John remained staunchly independent, making his films his way.

A few years later, the old guard became more accepting of his talent. The business was changing. The success of films like *Blow Up, Bonnie and Clyde, The Graduate, Who's Afraid of Virginia Wolf*, and, later, *Easy Rider* proved that audiences were ready for a new wave. As Arthur Penn, the director of *Bonnie and Clyde*, said about the new generation of filmmakers, "It wasn't just that we were sick of the system, the system was sick of itself." Old Hollywood had to adapt or die. John's film *Faces*, a cinéma-vérité study of a failing marriage, was nominated for three Academy Awards, including a Best Supporting Actor nomination for my friend Seymour Cassel.

I wanted to work in independent film to learn and grow as an actor, but Ray had positioned me as a movie star, and a role in a gritty, experimental film would tarnish that glossy image. He also gave a hard "no" when I was offered the role of a blind nurse in *The Devil at 4 O'Clock*. I was excited by the idea of working with Spencer Tracy, Frank Sinatra, and director Mervyn Leroy, but Ray had a definite sense of what I should and shouldn't do. Even a call from Frank Sinatra himself couldn't persuade him to change his mind.

And forget about television. One of the major networks approached Ray with the idea of basing a series on *Tamahine*. He dismissed the offer immediately, explaining to me that movie actors shouldn't do television. "Why should the public pay to see a star in a film when they can see her for free at home every week," he argued. Like many Hollywood producers and studio executives at the time, he viewed television as competition—a threat to box office—and discouraged his actors from crossing enemy lines.

I was open to all possibilities, but as long as I was under contract, I was bound by golden handcuffs, and they were starting to chafe.

An offer from Artur Brauner, an important German producer, to star in his film *The Corrupt Ones* prompted me to ask Ray to set me free. My contract was almost up, but the company would collect my fee if I accepted the offer while I was with Seven Arts. I discussed the situation with Ray. He was preoccupied with producing *Funny Girl* on Broadway and with the Herculean job of adapting the show into a film. Realistically, he couldn't devote much time to the career of one actress, so he agreed to release me.

I was grateful to Ray for discovering me and believing I had talent. Even though we ended our business arrangement, we maintained our friendship for decades until his death in 2004.

Then, at the ripe but not-so-old age of twenty-six, I was ready— no, *eager*—to experience independence and whatever came with it.

CHAPTER 13

If I wanted to change my image, I was off to a good start with *The Corrupt Ones*. In this fast-moving action/adventure film about the search for an ancient relic, Elke Sommer was the alluring object of Robert Stack's affection while I was the colorful villain, a classic Dragon Lady, albeit a very chic one. I prepared for the role by thinking about all the heavies I'd admired in other films. I discovered that, as with comedy, it's better not to lean into expectations. Instead of leading with my character's dark side, I played her as a disarming coquette, then gradually revealed my nefarious traits, including a penchant for torture. As Al Pacino wisely said in his film *The Devil's Advocate*, "Never let them see you coming." The best part about being a villain was that I could be more creative with the character.

We filmed at the Spandau Studios in West Berlin, but my memories of the Berlin Wall and the disturbing realities of life in East Berlin are what stay with me today. It was 1966, and the concrete barrier that separated West Berlin from East Berlin—the communist-controlled German Democratic Republic—looked like a prison wall. Armed guards patrolled the area day and night, their guns poised to shoot any would-be defectors. It was all so menacing.

I made plans with friends to go to the Brecht Theater in East Berlin to see a performance by the Berliner Ensemble, a theater company founded by playwright Bertolt Brecht and his wife, actress Helene Weigel. I was excited and nervous when we reached the checkpoint where we were required to surrender our passports before crossing the border (and maybe a little afraid that we wouldn't get them back). My first impression of East Berlin was what I had imagined. The streets were dimly lit and empty, and it looked downright depressing.

The atmosphere inside the theater was completely different. I don't speak German, so I couldn't understand what the actors were saying, but the ensemble's inventive use of music, costumes, sets, and lighting—a sharp contrast to the colorless world outside the theater—was so impressive that we immediately made plans to return for another performance.

The second time we went, things were different. Soldiers entered the theater during the performance and walked down the aisles with their guns drawn, searching for someone. Then, a man stood up, put his hands above his head in a sign of submission, and quietly surrendered to the soldiers, who marched him out of the theater. Not a word was spoken.

Later, I asked my friends about the incident. They shrugged and said these things happen in East Berlin.

I had an even more unsettling experience in West Berlin. One morning, I was on my way to the studio when I found a black rose on the floor outside my hotel room. I looked to see who might have left it, but no one was around. Why a black rose? It was ominous, like something out of a twisted fairy tale. I was afraid to take the elevator alone, so I called the front desk to ask for a security guard to escort me downstairs. After that, I was on edge, afraid I might find another black rose or worse.

When the film wrapped and I returned to Kühtai, Peter told me a man had been asking questions about me. Immediately, I thought of the black rose and came to the frightening conclusion that I had a stalker. Peter contacted the hotel manager where the mysterious man was staying, and they searched his room when he was out. They found a stash of medication prescribed for mental illness. Later, they spoke to the man, who told them he was a fan from Berlin. He had come to Kühtai to meet me. Peter convinced him that I was away visiting my family in Hong Kong, so he had no reason to stay. The man checked out of the hotel the following day.

This was the first time that I experienced the downside of celebrity. My interactions with enthusiastic fans had always been pleasant, but I couldn't stop thinking about this unstable—and potentially dangerous—admirer and his sinister black rose. I hoped I'd be able to shake off the feeling that I was being watched and might be vulnerable to the fantasies of a stranger. The man never tried to contact me again, but the experience opened my eyes to the difficulties of being a public figure. People think they know you because they've seen your larger-than-life image on-screen and have read all about you in newspapers and magazines. The chance that an overly enthusiastic fan could become a stalker is a disturbing possibility.

What I couldn't shake off when I returned from Berlin was the certainty that it was time to face a pressing problem at home. My marriage was failing, and I knew it was my fault. I was always away, working in far-off places. Spending a few weeks with Peter between films was no way to maintain a relationship. My father had warned me that these problems would come up—that I shouldn't rush into a marriage that had little chance of succeeding—but I didn't listen.

Now, I knew that he had given me good advice. But that's part of life. Making mistakes and learning lessons.

Peter and I didn't want to stay married and have separate lives, so the decision to divorce was mutual, and there was no drama or anger. The only issue was Bernie. Of course, I wanted him to live with me, but Peter would have to agree to that. Thankfully, and to his credit, Peter felt I should have custody of our son because I could give him a better and more interesting life than he would have in Austria.

Bernie and Ah Yee, my new family, needed a new home, and California seemed like the perfect place to start over. I rented a house in Laurel Canyon. I had lived in the canyon after filming *Flower Drum Song*, and I liked this woodsy, almost rural neighborhood in the Hollywood Hills. It felt remote and secluded even though it was only minutes from Sunset Boulevard.

When we moved there in 1967, however, I discovered that sleepy Laurel Canyon had become the American equivalent of London in 1963, an incubator for musicians with a brand-new sound and the maverick lifestyles that went with it. The canyon's signature scent, a blend of jasmine and eucalyptus, now included the headier aroma of marijuana.

Laurel Canyon had one main street, one store, one restaurant, and a who's who of residences belonging to (or rented by) rock royalty. Frank Zappa spent the summer of 1968 in a cavernous log cabin built by the Western movie star Tom Mix—until a never-ending influx of musician and groupie drop-ins prompted him to move to a more private house in the canyon on Woodrow Wilson Drive. Above our house in the hills was the home of Mama Cass of the Mamas and the Papas, who, true to her name, was a den mother and kept her front door open to her musician friends. Most doors were open. Everyone felt safe in this magical enclave, and the freewheeling interaction among musicians produced some of the era's signature songs.

At 8217 Lookout Mountain Avenue, Joni Mitchell wrote about "The Ladies of the Canyon," while her boyfriend Graham Nash described a special morning they shared at that location in "Our House." Jim Morrison wrote his hit song "Love Street" on the balcony of his rental on Rothdell Trail (which has since been renamed Love Street in his honor), describing the Canyon Country Store, where I shopped for last-minute groceries, as the place "where the creatures meet." Attached to the store was the Café Galleria, a small restaurant and coffee house that served everything from spaghetti and duck à l'orange to espresso. Morrison was right: all the locals gathered there, the biggest names on the Billboard charts—meaning any and all of *Crosby, Stills, & Nash*, Joni Mitchell, Michelle and John Phillips, Peter Tork of the *Monkees*, and Jackson Browne, to name a few—and the fans who came to be close to their idols.

It wasn't my world, but it was happening all around me, and I loved the canyon's casual lifestyle and laid-back atmosphere. Bernie played in our pool. I hung out with my old friends Seymour Cassel, and John Cassavetes and Gena Rowlands, who lived on Woodrow Wilson Drive, and with my Asian girlfriends from *Flower Drum Song*. I also started dating. I knew many actors, but I rarely dated them because, like Max, they tended to be self-absorbed. One of my boyfriends had a motorcycle, and I remember hanging onto him as we raced up and down the steep, winding roads that wrapped around the Hollywood Hills. We went a little too fast and crashed into a wall but walked away from the accident without a scratch. It was a charmed life.

Even work seemed like play. One of my first projects after my divorce was a two-episode pilot for the upcoming series *Hawaii Five-O*. Ray would have been horrified to hear I was doing *television*, but I couldn't see a single downside. We shot in Honolulu, Hawaii, one of my favorite places, the production had more staff than most feature films, and I got to work with Jack Lord, who championed the island and the islanders. Jack had creative control of the show and insisted it be shot on location. He also advocated hiring local actors for supporting roles, giving Pacific Islanders unprecedented opportunities. Twelve years later, *Hawaii Five-O* was the longest-running police drama in television history, making Jack a very wealthy man. When he died, he left his entire $40 million estate to Hawaiian charities.

Back home, I signed on for *The Wrecking Crew*, Dean Martin's fourth and final Matt Helm movie. In the series, he played a secret agent who constantly finds himself in life-threatening situations that usually involve bombs, fast cars, and an assortment of curvaceous bikinied women. Dean was so laid-back that even when staring at the business end of a gun, he looked like his biggest problem was deciding between a cocktail onion or an olive for his martini. His easygoing "Everybody Loves Somebody Sometime" persona fueled a successful recording, movie, and television career. *The Dean Martin Show*, in its fourth season, was a long-running hit for NBC, placing high in the ratings and winning Emmy and Golden Globe nominations.

I was cast as a sultry villainess with the double-entendre name, "U Rang." Elke Sommer played my blonde counterpart, and Sharon Tate co-starred as a schoolmarmish secret agent who became a beauty when she removed her glasses. We were in our twenties, while Dean was fifty-one, which was quite an age difference, but our characters were fair game for Matt Helm's not-so-subtle amorous advances.

I met Dean for the first time the day we started shooting. He walked onto the set holding a cup, and knowing his reputation for imbibing, I looked to see what he was drinking. He noticed and said, "No, no, it's not booze, it's just *tea*."

Dean had a great sense of humor and could joke about anything, like when he was supposed to introduce the three Matt Helm "girls" in a promotional spot. We lined up behind him, and he presented us one by one, saying, "Here's Elke Sommer, here's Sharon Tate, and here's Nancy Cohen, a nice Jewish girl." He got the laugh.

Sharon and I had a chance to spend time together when we were shooting on location in Palm Springs. She was beautiful inside and out—a free spirit who saw the good in everyone. She and Roman Polanski married in January, so she was a newlywed the summer we filmed. But to Sharon, everything was new. She had a wonderful naivete—a freshness—that was charming.

We were driving home from dinner one night when she spotted a hitchhiker in the distance. "Let's pick him up," she said. I looked at her as if she were crazy. We were on a dark, deserted road—not a light or a sign of life—only this *man*, a stranger who could have been a killer as far as I was concerned. "No, *no*, we can't do that," I told her, eager to see the last of him in the rearview mirror. She tried again, pleading, "Oh, come on, Nancy," probably thinking he was tired and desperate for a ride. That was Sharon—kind and generous. I don't think she had a mean bone in her body. Apparently, *I* did because I didn't give in, and we drove right past him.

Sharon and I had a kung fu–themed fight scene in the film, so the director brought in a young martial arts expert to choreograph our moves. Enter Bruce Lee. Bruce, I discovered, was more than a fight coordinator. He was an actor who had appeared in over twenty films in our native Hong Kong and had recently starred as Kato, the Green Hornet's sidekick, in the television series. He taught martial arts to some of the biggest stars in Hollywood, including Steve McQueen, but these credentials only told part of Bruce's story, which he shared with me—in Cantonese—as we got to know each other on the set.

Bruce was born in San Francisco. He was the son of an actor who came to the United States on an extended visa with his Chinese theater troupe. His family moved back to their native Hong Kong when he was an infant, and Bruce grew up in Kowloon, not far from where I lived. He was so physically active as a child that his family called him "Never sits still." When he was six, he started acting in Hong Kong films, using the name "Little Dragon Li." Later, he attended La Salle, a religious school I knew well because the boys frequently came to Maryknoll to flirt with the girls when I was a student there.

Bruce became interested in martial arts like so many other young men in Hong Kong in the 1950s. He was drawn to wing chun, a form of combat that emphasized fluidity and control: Practitioners had to be shapeshifting, like water. Not surprisingly, he was also an extraordinary dancer and excelled at the cha-cha. Bruce saw a connection between the wing chun moves and the Latin dance and practiced his steps to the point where he entered a big dance competition and won. He loved telling people he was once crowned the "Cha-Cha Champion of Hong Kong."

There were times when Bruce's fists got him into trouble. On one occasion, he picked a fight with the wrong person, a young man from a well-connected family. They threatened harsh legal consequences for the fight, prompting Bruce's parents to send him back to the United States, where he still held citizenship. He told me that if he had stayed in Hong Kong, he probably would have joined a gang and been knifed to death. Instead, he went to California, enrolled in college, and determined to make something of himself—maybe even become a dentist.

Ironically, Bruce moved to San Francisco to start his new life in 1959, the same year *I* arrived in Hollywood. Bruce followed a different path from the one he imagined. He developed a reputation as a kung fu expert and met Jay Sebring, Hollywood's most flamboyant and influential hairdresser. One of Sebring's clients, a producer named William Dozier, was looking for a Chinese James Bond for one of his projects. Sebring introduced him to Bruce, and while that project never happened, Dozier placed Bruce under contract and ultimately cast him as Kato. He also arranged for him to take acting lessons with my teacher, Jeff Corey, another connection we shared.

The television series was short-lived, but Bruce had a wife and a young son to support, so teaching martial arts to celebrities and Hollywood insiders, including writer Sterling Silliphant, paid the bills. He pointed out that when he first came to America, he had only a hundred dollars in his pocket and couldn't afford anything, not even reading glasses. Ten years later, he owned a house in Bel Air and a Porsche and was *very* excited about the future. His goal was to return to Hong Kong to become a big martial arts star. But he was also developing a project that might make him a celebrity in America. Either way, he was sure he would be famous. He was such a positive person that I believed him!

Bruce was an excellent teacher when we worked on the fight scene. Sharon and I learned how to make our moves look convincing without hurting each other. Bruce approached the sequence as if it were a ballet with combat. I'd kick, and Sharon would spin. She'd push me away, and I'd attack from behind. Sharon had the advantage of wearing pants, but I wore a Pucci mini dress that bared so much leg that every high kick threatened to reveal all. I enjoyed getting to know Bruce and Sharon and watching Dean's never-break-a-sweat approach to comedy. Sharon became friends with Bruce, too, and introduced him to Roman, who started taking lessons in martial arts and self-defense.

I went from this whimsical, cocktail-infused spy caper to *The McMasters*, a gritty Western. Why a Western? Filmmakers in the late 1960s were drawn to the classic genre because they found parallels among the frontier setting, the war in Vietnam, and contemporary racial conflicts and portrayed the Old West through this revisionist lens. Sam Peckinpah's *The Wild Bunch*, Arthur Penn's *Little Big Man*, Ralph Nelson's *Soldier Blue*, Robert Altman's *McCabe and Mrs. Miller*, and George Roy Hill's *Butch Cassidy and the Sundance Kid* were Westerns with a modern sensibility and a conscience.

The McMasters, which we filmed in 1969, takes place immediately after the Civil War and tells the story of a Black Union soldier's painful reentry into a hostile world that rejects him because of his color and his romantic relationship with my character, a Native American woman. My co-stars were the formidable Brock Peters, David Carradine, John Carradine, Jack Palance, and Burl Ives.

I viewed the role as a valuable acting exercise because I was stripped of the niceties that enhanced my performances in other films. No Irene Sharaff. No Vidal Sassoon. My hair was long and tangled, my face was streaked with dirt, and my costumes were minimalist (aka *rags*). The glamorous Nancy Kwan was nowhere to be seen, although audiences did see most of me in my very first nude scene. I agreed to do it because it wasn't gratuitous—my character needed to bathe in the scene, and it was an important, transformational moment for her as she transitioned from outdoor tribal life to her new home and different customs.

I wanted to *push* my boundaries, knowing I would learn from the experience. The film was raw and violent because it was meant to reflect the violence of our times, a reality that hit closer to home that summer.

In August, exactly one year after we finished *The Wrecking Crew*, my pleasant memories of the shoot were shattered by an unimaginable tragedy. Sharon Tate and her friends—Jay Sebring, Abigail Folger, and Voytek Frykowski—were murdered at her house on Cielo Drive in nearby Benedict Canyon. The slaughter of this transcendent young woman who only saw *good* was unfathomable...and terrifying. Any of us who knew Sharon might have been there that night. She welcomed all her friends to drop by her house—that was the relaxed California way.

But Sharon's murder and the brutal LaBianca killings that immediately followed marked a dramatic shift in how we lived. Suddenly, our secluded canyon homes seemed so vulnerable. Open doors slammed shut and were fortified with locks and security systems. Some people purchased guns. I was alone with

Bernie because Ah Yee had returned to Hong Kong for a visit. Nighttime was the worst—I walked from room to room checking the windows. I used to love the house's openness to the world outside. Now, I just felt exposed and unsafe.

For the next two months, the police tried to solve the case. There were no answers, only questions. Could the killer have been one of Sharon's friends? Someone we knew? Fear made us suspicious of everyone. One of the more bizarre theories came to light years later in 1985, when Roman Polanski revealed in his autobiography that, at his most paranoid, he had foolishly suspected Bruce Lee of killing Sharon.

They became friends when Bruce was training Roman. After Sharon's murder, but before the killer was found, Bruce casually mentioned to Roman that he had lost his glasses. Roman remembered that a pair of glasses had been found at the crime scene. At the time, he was so desperate to find any clue to the killings that he measured the lenses for their prescription, hoping the information would help to identify the killer. When Roman heard that Bruce's glasses were missing, he assumed the worst and offered to take him to the optometrist to buy him new glasses, secretly planning to compare Bruce's prescription to the one he had. Of course, the prescriptions didn't match, and Roman realized that poor Bruce was innocent.

Bruce died before Roman published his book. I'm happy he never knew his grief-stricken friend had suspected him.

CHAPTER 14

In October, the police arrested Charles Manson for suspected auto theft and determined his connection to the Tate-LaBianca murders. Somehow, the evil that had a name, a face, and a motive was less frightening than fear of the unknown, so I stopped worrying about random threats and settled back into my routine with Bernie. I did try to teach him to be cautious about strangers because he was a very friendly and trusting child.

So trusting that I came home one day to find a man—an absolute stranger—in my living room. *Wait*, I thought. *I recognize him*. He was Warren Oates, a character actor who was all over television and had starred with Bill Holden in Sam Peckinpah's classic film *The Wild Bunch*. And there he was, sitting on my couch. Bernie was so enthusiastic about our uninvited guest that it was difficult to understand his explanation.

There must have been a misunderstanding about pick-up time at school because when I didn't show up, Bernie happily got into a car belonging to another parent. He justified doing so because he said the stranger's car looked just like mine, and, as he found out, the man was an actor, just like me. Since we had so much in common, Bernie was sure it was okay.

Warren was lovely, and we laughed at Bernie's thought process. Then I got serious. No riding in cars with strangers, *ever*. The hardest part of being a parent is to think of the crazy things your child might do and tell them not to do it. Staying one step ahead of Bernie, who was smart in two languages, was a full-time job.

It was around this time that a mutual friend at Warner Bros. introduced me to a young writer named David Giler, the son of Bernie Giler, a successful screen and television writer. David grew up in Hollywood, where he attended Hollywood High School and knew everyone. He had made a name for himself by writing episodes of several popular television series, including *The Man from U.N.C.L.E.* and *Burke's Law*. Then, he got his big break—an assignment to write his first feature film—but it turned out to be such a disaster that it almost ended his promising career.

Myra Breckinridge, a satirical novel written by Gore Vidal in 1968, landed in Hollywood at the very moment when the industry's traditionally prudish rating system expanded to accommodate films with adult content. The fact that the challenging story centered around a transgender woman who sets out to upend the star system in sexually explicit ways didn't stop Twentieth Century Fox from paying almost a million dollars for the movie rights and hiring David to write the script.

The film, which starred Raquel Welch, Rex Reed, Mae West, the venerable John Huston, and newcomer Farah Fawcett, received an X rating and a tidal wave of publicity *and* was universally loathed, prompting *Time* magazine to describe it as being "about as funny as a child molester." Fortunately for David, most of the criticism rained on the source material and the director, Michael Sarne.

When I met David, he was working at Warner Bros., where a forward-thinking executive named John Calley had given a group of hot, up-and-coming screenwriters contracts and a weekly salary to come up with the next *Easy Rider*, the surprise counterculture hit that forced Hollywood to leap into the youth market. Like Ray Stark, who plucked Francis Ford Coppola from film school, Calley was investing in the next generation. "When formulas break down in times of uncertainty, it's a breeding ground for young talent," he explained. "Everyone is ready to listen to wilder forms and concepts. We're inclined to take enlightened gambles on young people."

The "young people" in the Warner Bros. think tank included David, John Milius, Walter Hill (who later became David's partner at their company, Brandywine), Brian De Palma, Terence Malik, and other "young turks." They saw themselves as the bad boys, the rulebreakers, the *new* Hollywood.

David was charming and funny, and there was immediate chemistry between us. The very next day, he sent me a beautiful basket of flowers (a courtly *old* Hollywood move) and asked me to go out with him. I hesitated because of his age—he was a young, Peter Pan–ish twenty-six while I was a mature thirty-one—but I decided it wouldn't hurt me to have a little fun.

Did I say a little fun? David was all about fun. I have never been out with anyone who had such zest for life. He loved nothing more than to party with his friends, usually his fellow writers and filmmakers. He'd have a drink in one hand, a cigarette in the other, and an endless supply of stories to tell. His writer's mind was curious about everything. He watched as Ah Yee and I played Mahjong and instantly mastered the game. He had a quick intellect and a good sense of humor. Bernie liked him. Even Ah Yee was won over because David always complimented her cooking.

David's energy and enthusiasm were contagious, and our relationship progressed quickly. We got so caught up in our whirlwind romance that he impulsively proposed to me. I didn't really want to get married, but David could be very persuasive. Eventually, he talked me into it.

David's mother and sisters were in Bel Air, so it would have made sense to get married in Los Angeles. But in David's mind, even a wedding had to be an adventure. He wanted to move quickly before I changed my mind, so off we went to Carson City, Nevada (no blood tests, no waiting period), where we were married by Justice of the Peace Pete Supera, who, coincidentally, had married Barbra Streisand and Elliot Gould, and Bruce Dern and his wife, Andrea Beckett. The three-minute ceremony was almost as short as my mini-skirt. *Time* magazine ran an item about our elopement, describing me as the "sloe-eyed Eurasian actress" and David as a "Hollywood scriptwriter, whose most recent credit, *if that is the term*, is Myra Breckinridge." The stink of that movie followed poor David everywhere, even to his own wedding!

I avoided telling my father my plans (am I seeing a pattern here?), waiting until *after* the ceremony to give him the news. "Big daughter" was too old to get into trouble, but I could hear the disapproval in his voice, and I quickly arranged a "meet the parents" trip to Hong Kong.

Thank goodness Daddy didn't ask me to marry in Christ Church this time. I had no desire to walk down another aisle. We spent a few weeks at home with the family. Bernie, the only grandchild, was the center of attention, and David scored points by playing Mahjong with my stepmother and her friends.

It wasn't until we were back in Los Angeles that I felt the impact of the expression, "Marry in haste, repent in leisure." My best-case scenario for our marriage was that I would have a partner whose company I enjoyed, and Bernie would have a father figure in his life. He had little to no contact with Peter—Austria could have been another planet—and I worried about Bernie growing up without a paternal influence.

But there was nothing paternal about David, and the behavior that was fun in a boyfriend was not ideal for a husband or a father. When we started living together as a family, the differences in our lifestyles became more apparent. David still liked to go out and party hard with his friends, while I wanted to stay home and spend time with Bernie. The fact that David was at the center of young Hollywood's notoriously drug-fueled culture didn't help. Cocaine and marijuana were the tools of the trade for the young, hip, and ambitious. Maybe drugs made them feel smarter, edgier, and more creative, but they weren't for me, and I definitely didn't want them around my son.

We enjoyed some good times together, especially during the periods when David was fully functional. The British director Jack Clayton (who later helmed the big-budget Robert Redford and Mia Farrow version of *The Great Gatsby*) was in preproduction on *Casualties of War*, a film based on a true story about the court martial of four American soldiers accused of committing atrocities in Vietnam. The project was in jeopardy because Clayton was unhappy with writer Pete Hamill's script. Then, it was assigned to David, who started working on it right after our wedding.

Two months later, David delivered a script Clayton regarded as "magnificent." It was gripping, disturbing, and provocative in its exploration of the horrors of war. We went to London to spend time with Jack and his wife, Haya Harareet; for me, a happy return to a city I loved, and for David, a meaningful validation of his talent. Clayton never made the film because the story was considered too controversial at the time. It wasn't until 1989 that Brian De Palma directed a version by David Rabe, but the David Giler screenplay of *Casualties of War* lives on in legend.

David was also working on *The Black Bird*, a script about Sam Spade's son, Sam Spade, Jr., and his continuing adventures with the Maltese Falcon. He wrote a wonderful role for me—a complex character who could be a heroine or a villain, and I was excited about the film's possibilities.

Good times aside, David and I realized we weren't the best match. He would never settle down, and I would never be a party girl. We separated amicably and later filed for divorce in 1972.

The question was, what should I do next? I could stay in Los Angeles, but I was disenchanted with my life there, and not only because of my ill-fated marriage. I loved acting, but the Hollywood landscape was difficult for any actor to navigate and doubly difficult for an Asian actor. In 1961, *Flower Drum Song* seemed to signal wider acceptance and new opportunities for Asians in the entertainment business. But ten years later, we were still facing the same prejudices. I say "we" because without Seven Arts, I was no longer offered roles that were race blind. I might be the first name on a producer's list for a role that called for a woman to be "exotic" in some way, like the Native American in *The McMasters*, but I wasn't cast as the girl next door.

I had a conversation about the realities of Hollywood with my friend Bruce Lee right before he went to Hong Kong to work on *The Big Boss*, a martial arts movie produced by Raymond Chow.

Bruce told me he was happy about *The Big Boss*, but he was more excited about two possible projects at Warner Brothers. One was *Kung Fu*, a television series about a Shaolin monk and martial arts expert in the Old West, and the other was *The Warrior*, a series Bruce had developed with his friend Sterling Silliphant, also about the adventures of a Chinese martial arts master in the Old West.

Bruce was optimistic about both projects and expected to hear good news from the studio. I listened to him go on about it for a while, not wanting to dampen his enthusiasm. Finally, I said to him, "It's not going to happen. Hollywood is not ready to have a Chinaman on television in their homes every week." Bruce looked at me for a moment, surprised by my candor. "I bet you ten dollars I get the role," he challenged. That was Bruce, always positive.

My words must have made an impression on him, however, because a short time later, a reporter asked him about his prospects in Hollywood, and Bruce answered, "Hollywood is trying to decide if the American television audience is ready for an Oriental hero."

Bruce completed *The Big Boss*, and it delivered a kung fu chop across the globe when it opened to historic box office on November 21, 1971, pulling in a million dollars in one weekend. Suddenly, Bruce was a hero in Hong Kong, a local boy who made it, a symbol of Chinese power, and an inspiration to his countrymen who, as subjects in a colony, were used to living in the shadow of presumed British superiority.

I hope Bruce's overnight success softened the blow when Warner Bros. told him he had not been cast in *Kung Fu*, and they were passing on *The Warrior*.

Publicly, studio executives suggested that Bruce's aggressive fighting style was wrong for the character "Caine" in *Kung Fu*. Caine was a meditative man who used his fists as a last resort, unlike Bruce, who was always ready to dance into combat. What they told each other in private, however, was that Bruce was *too* authentic, that he was short and had a heavy accent—coded ways of saying that he was too Chinese.

David Carradine won the role and, incredibly, considering it was 1971, would do it in yellowface. The Association of Asian Pacific American Artists, headed by veteran actor James Hong (who played the nightclub headwaiter in *Flower Drum Song* and most recently played the grandfather in *Everything Everywhere All at Once*), protested this step backward with a formal complaint, demanding that an Asian actor play Caine and a Chinese historical consultant oversee the production to ensure its authenticity. This being Hollywood, a compromise was the only possible resolution. Sure, the producers were willing to hire a consultant, but they held firm on casting Carradine.

In the end, the AAPAA backed down from the fight because, as James Hong explained, "As the show went on, we realized it was a great source of employment for the Asian acting community." It was better to have opportunities, even if it meant sacrificing ideals. *Kung Fu* became a huge hit that kept Asian actors busy for three seasons. James Hong had a role in the *Kung Fu* pilot, and *Flower Drum Song* veterans Benson Fong and James Shigeta appeared in subsequent episodes. I co-starred with David Carradine in a special two-part episode called "The Cenotaph" during season two.

As for *The Warrior*...well, it was obvious that Warner Bros. couldn't produce *two* television shows about a roving martial arts expert in the Old West. Flash forward to 2019 when Cinemax debuted the series *Warrior*, based on Bruce's original material and produced by his daughter, Shannon Lee. As Bruce hoped, the series, which ran for three seasons, was very popular, and it was nominated for two Emmy Awards, including Best Stunt Coordination.

Conspiracy theories abound about Bruce's connection to *Kung Fu*. His wife, Linda, and his fans believe that the series evolved from his ideas about a Western-themed story of a Kung Fu warrior. But *Kung Fu* writers Ed Spielman and Howard Friedlander counter that they wrote a treatment for a feature film about the same subject, and that became the source material for *Kung Fu*. Bruce never commented, so it remains a mystery.

I'm sorry to say I won the ten-dollar bet, but Bruce didn't lose anything. His long-held dream of being an international martial arts star had come true. He had a platform and a mission. "It's about time we had an Oriental hero," he told the press. "Never mind some guy bouncing around the country in a pigtail or something. I have to be a real human being. No cook. No laundryman."

Bruce found everything he always wanted in Hong Kong. Now, I decided, it was time for me to return home. The pressing reason was that my father had been diagnosed with cancer. We didn't know how much time he had left, but I wanted to be there for him. I also wondered what it would be like to actually *live* in Hong Kong, the way Ka Shen, my younger self, might have lived had I opened a ballet school instead of going to my uncle's studio on the fateful day when Suzie Wong changed the course of my life. I had such happy memories of my childhood.

Would I feel the same way as an adult? There was only one way to find out.

My agent thought moving to Hong Kong was a *terrible* idea. "You can't go back," he said, warning that he wouldn't be able to get me work. It would be a bad career move. Honestly, I wasn't worried about my career. I had been working steadily since I was nineteen, and I was tired of feeling powerless in a system that was stacked against me, where there were limitations on the roles I could play and barriers that never seemed to move.

What if I had listened to the manager who told me to get an abortion when I was pregnant with Bernie? *That* bad career move was the best decision I ever made. Not that it was really a decision because I never for one second considered giving up my child for a role in a film.

And contrary to what my agent thought, Hollywood wasn't the center of the universe.

Coincidentally, I had just attended a screening of an independent film called *Sidekickers*, later known as *Five the Hard Way*. It was pretty violent in that low-budget, B-picture way, but when I met producer Ross Hagen and he described his experiences making the film, he spoke about his work with such passion and enthusiasm that he almost convinced me it was a masterpiece. I also met his wife, Claire.

Ross called me the next day with an offer. He was planning to shoot his new film, *Wonder Woman*, in the Philippines and thought I'd be perfect for the role of Dr. Tzu. It was a good opportunity, and I would be with people who loved making movies. So much for not getting any work. Hong Kong was looking promising already.

But I wasn't thinking only of myself. I was certain that moving to Hong Kong would be good for Bernie. I wanted him to spend time with my father, to connect with his heritage, and to experience the world of my childhood—where I joyfully collected my red envelopes on Chinese New Year, explored the street markets, and was the fearless Flying Hen of Homantin Hill.

I had made up my mind. We were going home.

CHAPTER 15

Everything fell into place when we arrived in Hong Kong. I found an apartment on the Kowloon Side and enrolled Bernie in a nearby English school. He was so happy to be with "Gung Gung," as he called my father. Cancer was taking its toll on Daddy, and he was in and out of the hospital, but he always cheered up at the sight of his high-spirited grandson. They'd curl up together and watch television—even the simplest pastimes were meaningful because time was not my father's friend.

As I expected, Bernie, a precocious nine-year-old, had no trouble adjusting to Hong Kong. I was always amused to watch people's reactions when they saw him on the street. They stopped to stare at this blond-haired, blue-eyed angelic child who looked like he had been airlifted from the beaches of sunny California and commented to each other in Chinese about his unusual appearance, not realizing that he knew *exactly* what they were saying.

One day, when Bernie and I were shopping on Nathan Road in Kowloon, a woman stared at *me* and started carrying on about my freckles. "Leave my mother alone," Bernie shouted at her in Chinese. The woman looked at Bernie, shocked. "That foreign devil boy speaks Chinese," she said incredulously as she quickly backed away. Bernie thought it was funny, like having a superpower.

I spent time with my family and caught up with old friends, including Bruce, who was working on *Fist of Fury*, his second martial arts movie for Raymond Chow. When I visited him on the set, he swaggered over to me—bare-chested and looking leaner and stronger than I'd ever seen him. "Punch me," he said, pointing to his steel abdomen. I hit him a few times, but he wasn't impressed. "Harder," he urged. I really gave it my best shot. "That's all you can do?" he laughed.

He was proud to show me his office at the studio, a symbol of his success. Tucked away on a bookshelf was a reminder of the lean years. Bruce had kept his broken eyeglasses; the ones he told me he couldn't afford to replace when he was a college student in San Francisco. If *Fist of Fury* made as much money as *The Big Boss*, he would be able to buy anything he wanted.

Flash forward to a few months later, when *Fist of Fury* opened at the Queen's Theater in Hong Kong. The audience was so excited to see Bruce in action that they cheered and ripped out the seats. The movie went on to make $100 million, which would be $746 million at the time of this writing. What's more, Warner Bros. came back, hat in hand, with an offer for Bruce to star in an international coproduction of *Enter the Dragon*. Bruce went shopping.

Bernie was still young enough to take time off from school, so he accompanied me to the Philippines when I shot Ross Hagen's *Wonder Woman*. Normally, I would say that travel is educational, but our movements were so restricted in the Philippines, a country where Ferdinand and Imelda Marcos reigned with martial law, that Bernie spent most of his time at the hotel and on the set. He was content because he loved ordering room service, and when he came to work with me, he was the star attraction. Ross and Claire, who quickly became my close friends, doted on him, as did the cast and crew.

Bernie loved to tell jokes but was terrible at it because he started laughing before he delivered the punch line. Our friends listened patiently and always laughed with him. He was so adorable that people were happy to indulge him.

Here's what I learned when I made *Wonder Woman.* The money was good, but there were more important benefits. Ross had figured out a way to produce movies inexpensively in Southeast Asia. I liked being able to work close to Hong Kong at a time when I needed to be near my father and make a real home for Bernie, and I also liked working with friends. After so many years of making my career a priority, I was determined to find a way to balance life and work, and Ross's independent productions gave me security and independence. I decided I would do more of them in the future.

My life in Hong Kong took an interesting—and unexpected—turn when I received an invitation from the Chinese government to visit China, a country that was usually closed to outsiders in 1972. I instantly accepted the invitation to visit film studios and other cultural institutions because I saw a rare opportunity to explore this enormous country that had been cloaked in mystery since World War II. I had lived in China as a child during the Japanese occupation of Hong Kong, but I was so young that my memories were visceral ones of fear, hunger, and illness. Now, I would have a chance to see China with adult eyes and get to know the people.

A friend who had connections in China helped me to secure a visa (which was difficult to obtain even with my official invitation), and a two-week trip was planned. I had three priorities—to visit the Shanghai Film Studio, the Beijing ballet school, and the Kwan Village, the home of my ancestors, the Kwan Clan, in Poon Yu near Guangzhou.

President Richard Nixon was planning to make his historic first trip to China in February, but I got there first, which apparently made me a "person of interest" to the CIA. I later discovered that agents were tracking my moves and listed my name in the CIA report *Appearance and Activities of Leading Personalities of the People's Republic of China*

PEKING NCNA—E 16 JAN72 F—11 NCNA—E 28JAN72
F—20 28/01/72 RECD US ACTRESS **NANCY KWAN**
POSITION: HEAD, CUL GRP, STATE COUNCIL

On January 12, 1972, I took the train from Hong Kong to Lo Wu, where I disembarked and proceeded to walk across a bridge to the city of Shenzhen, the standard way of entering China. Crossing the border on foot, like a traveler from a previous century, heightened my feeling that I was moving into an unfamiliar world. It was a sensory experience, unlike the antiseptic you-could-be-anywhere process of departing from one airport and arriving at another.

I surrendered my passport at the border security checkpoint, just as I did when I visited East Berlin. Perhaps naively, I didn't think about whether the trip was dangerous in any way, although several people raised that question about China when I told them where I was going. "I'm just curious," I told them. As an artist and an Asian, I wanted to learn more about Chinese culture and history.

I was met at the border by a young woman about my age, a

graduate of Beijing University. She introduced herself as Chang Mao and explained she would be my interpreter and traveling companion for the duration of the trip. Mao was lovely and very efficient. She focused on making sure that our visits to Canton, Shanghai, Hangzhou, Nanking, and Peking ran smoothly.

The trip was a blur of planned activities, some more memorable than others. I kept a journal (where I wrote a staggering number of detailed notes about Chinese history) covering the highlights of my visit. At the Shanghai Ballet Company, I attended two ballets that were considered classics of revolutionary China—*The White Haired Girl*, the country's first "opera" ballet, and *Red Detachment of Women*. Both ballets depicted the miserable lives of the oppressed classes before the Cultural Revolution—*and* their happiness after. I met the dancers and learned that most of their teachers were Russian-trained. We had an interesting chat about how the company mixed traditional Chinese ballet with Western ballet.

We also visited the Shanghai Film Studio, and my first impression was that it was frozen in time. The filmmakers still used large old-fashioned movie cameras imported from Russia, and the actors wore way too much makeup, suitable for the stage but not for film. While the people I met had not seen my films because they weren't exhibited in China, they were curious about how we made movies in Hollywood. I demonstrated a more modern approach, showing them how to apply makeup in a way that would look more natural.

When I discussed techniques with the actors, I discovered that we had a lot in common, especially in the ways we prepared for films. A young actress who was starring in a new film about medical workers in China's remote countryside told me she spent time in a rural area to research her role. We agreed that experience was the best teacher. Even though we came from different worlds, there were no barriers between us when we talked about our craft.

Mao and I moved quickly from one location to the next, and I found beauty in every city. I loved the way the clock atop Shanghai's historic Customs House chimed "The East Is West," China's national anthem, every hour.

In Nanjing, I stopped to visit Dr. Sun Yat-Sen's Mausoleum and remembered that my great-grandparents' house in Hong Kong, the city he described as his "intellectual birthplace," had been his home away from home.

The Dragon Well Tea Commune in Hangzhou was a magical place. Believed to be the home of ancient dragons, it became the source of Dragon Well Tea, famous for its magical and medicinal properties. The water in the commune's namesake well was so buoyant and rich in minerals that even heavy coins could float on the top. And the gardens! I saw square bamboo, something I had never seen before, and ponds filled with enormous carp that shimmered in vibrant shades of orange. Surprisingly, the fish were hundreds of years old.

The city of Ancient Hangzhou, which Marco Polo described as "beyond dispute the finest and noblest city in the world," was a tranquil refuge of scenic gardens, bridges, waterways, and islands. We arrived during the off-season, so we were the only guests at the hotel. But Chang Mao was so strict about observing protocol that she always declined my invitations to sit with me at dinner. She must have been advised to keep her distance from the foreigner, so, even in an empty hotel dining room, I sat alone at a table on one side of the restaurant while she sat alone at another.

THE WORLD OF NANCY KWAN

It seemed silly to me, but she was not the kind of person who would ever think of bending or breaking a rule.

I marveled at the treasures in the Forbidden City, where I wandered through rooms filled with antiquities. I was admiring some jade when a man introduced himself. He was George Wald, a Harvard professor (and winner of the Nobel Prize in physiology and medicine in 1967) and a noted pacifist who was visiting China for several weeks and then traveling to North Vietnam to meet with prisoners of war. Like me, his only mission on this day was to appreciate the beauty of the Forbidden City, and we enjoyed doing it together.

In Peking (now Beijing), a government official named Wu The, the head of the cultural group sponsoring my visit, introduced me to dignitaries from various literary and art circles. I also attended the opera, rode the subway, toured factories, and observed a class at a ballet school. The dancers were fabulous! I remember having dinner at a restaurant that served only duck— we started with duck soup, duck *this*, duck *that*, and the finale, Peking Duck.

I stood at the Great Wall of China wrapped in a fur-lined coat because the weather was freezing in January. A woman ran over to give me some advice. "Coat on wrong way," she said, gesturing that the fur should be on the outside. I explained that the fur belonged on the inside, but she insisted otherwise, telling me, "Not good." She was trying to be helpful, but she was so persistent that it was funny.

My interpreter was very helpful because her translation skills were strong. However, she had learned "book" English, meaning that she understood the literal meanings of words without knowing the right way to use them. To express how much she enjoyed our conversations, she said, "I love having intercourse with a foreigner." I looked at her for a moment, then burst out laughing— and set her straight before she said it to another foreigner!

Early on in my trip, I had asked my government handlers to find the Kwan Village. So many locations in China had been renamed that it was difficult to determine exactly where it was. I didn't want to disappoint Daddy, so I was so relieved when they finally found it and arranged for me to go there. The entire village, about three hundred men, women, and children, turned out to greet me. They applauded and laughed good-naturedly at their Kwan relative from outer space. After the older Kwan members made speeches, we sat down to a meal of local vegetables, nuts, dried fruits, and fish. Some of the Kwans were farmers, but most looked after the nearby fishponds.

Spending time with them brought back memories of the Kwan legends I heard as a child. One of the most recognizable images from ancient Chinese history is that of Guan Yu, a Chinese warrior who lived during the Han Dynasty. He has a red face and a long beard, and he's holding a guandao, a Chinese pole weapon. His picture can be found in every police station— and weirdly in every massage parlor and brothel—in Hong Kong because he was a strong, righteous man who became the symbol of justice. His story is chronicled in the book *The Three Kingdoms*.

According to legend, in ancient times, Guan Yu and his men raided what is now the Kwan Clan village during a dynastic turf war. Normally, a warlord would slaughter everyone, but during this battle, Guan Yu came across a pregnant woman, felt a stirring of sympathy, and ordered his men to spare her. Unfortunately, his act of mercy led to his downfall. The woman's child grew up to become a great warrior named Sun Quan (as in Kwan), who killed Guan Yu. I couldn't wait to tell my father about my visit and the memories it rekindled.

When it was time for me to leave China, my journey ended where it began, at the Lo Wu Bridge. My passport was returned to me. I said goodbye to Chang Mao, who demurred when I asked for her address so I could send her a thank-you note—communication with outsiders was discouraged—and I walked to the train that would take me home to Hong Kong. The experience was the same as it had been two weeks earlier, but I was different. History had come alive for me, and my interactions with so many different people, from the dancers at the ballet and the actors at the studio to my distant relatives in the Kwan village, confirmed my belief that borders don't define human nature. Wherever we are, we are all the same.

Even the movie business knew no borders. Hong Kong in 1972 was Hollywood East, seven thousand miles away from Los Angeles, but with a similar caste system and its share of rivalries and backstage dramas.

The studio hierarchy was topped by Run Run Shaw at the Shaw Brothers Studio, and Raymond Chow at his company, Golden Harvest. Run Run was a classic movie mogul along the lines of Louis B. Mayer at MGM and Jack Warner at Warner Brothers. He saw himself as an empire builder when he opened Shaw Movietown, a studio facility in Hong Kong's Clearwater Bay, in 1961. There, he produced most of the films in Asia. When asked about his favorite films, Run Run famously said, "I particularly like the movies that make money." He also had the foresight to open TVB, a television station that produced Chinese language programs.

Run Run had the Midas touch and was particularly successful at making and distributing films made in the wuxia tradition, an early form of kung fu. The first wuxia stories date back to 300 BC, when tales were told about soldiers of fortune, or mercenaries, who dedicated themselves to feudal lords. Over time, this protagonist evolved to be a principled young hero—skilled in martial arts—who embarks on a quest for justice and enlightenment. Often, the wuxia hero has superhuman qualities and can fly or defy gravity in some way (for a contemporary version, think of the characters in Ang Lee's *Crouching Tiger, Hidden Dragon*, or Quentin Tarantino's *Kill Bill*).

Run Run was so successful at producing movies that were traditional in their storytelling—costume dramas, musicals, and classic martial arts films—that he was slow to recognize the potential (or value) of an exciting kung fu upstart, Bruce Lee.

If Run Run was Hong Kong's version of Warner Brothers, Raymond Chow was early Miramax—the scrappy independent who quickly became the little engine that *could*. Raymond began his career at the Shaw Brothers Studio in 1958 but struck out to start his own company in 1970. Initially, Golden Harvest produced standard action films until, unlike Run Run, Raymond said yes to Bruce Lee and cast him as the star of *The Big Boss*.

During his time in Hollywood, Bruce learned new techniques that made his kung fu moves look better on camera. He knew which kicks and punches worked best on film and how to position the camera for maximum impact. Traditional Chinese martial arts movies gave each fight scene equal weight and filmed every conflict at length, which resulted in a slow-moving story.

Bruce struggled to make his point to the unreceptive director of *The Big Boss*, but ultimately, Raymond realized that Bruce was right to want to reinvent the genre for a modern audience. He let Bruce do it his way and reaped the real "golden harvest" when *The Big Boss* and *Fist of Fury* were blockbusters.

Both Run Run and Raymond approached me about working together. Run Run invited me to visit him at Shaw Bothers and gave me the star treatment. He sent a car so I wouldn't have to drive, personally escorted me around the studio, and introduced me to some of the actors working on the set. Over tea, he made a generous offer. He wanted to make a film with me, any film I liked, and he would provide a writer to develop the script. How could I refuse? Run Run had the money—and the power—to make anything happen.

But Hong Kong's preeminent producer had second thoughts after I went to China. The post–World War II rivalry between Mao Tse Tung's communist government in Mainland China and Chiang Kai-Shek's Republic of China in Taiwan had to be factored into business decisions because appearing to favor one could lead to trouble with the other. Run Run called me with bad news and an apology. He wanted to work with me, but my trip to China might be viewed unfavorably by Taiwan, and that market was too important for him to jeopardize. Regretfully, he had to cancel our agreement.

While it was hard to imagine that the travels of one actress could have such a significant ripple effect, I understood Run Run's concerns. Did I regret going to China because it cost me the deal? Not at all. The memory of any film we might have made together would fade in time, but the experiences I had in China will always be with me.

And life is such that when a door closes, another opens. A few months later, I received an offer from Edward J. N. Ho, an independent producer in Hong Kong. He knew about my visit to China but wanted to work with me. The film was *Spring Comes Not Again*, a dramatic story about love and betrayal. I accepted his offer because I thought the role of Betty, a woman caught up in an intensely emotional situation that leads to her suicide, was strong and provocative (the kind of role I had longed to play in Hollywood), and Ho had signed Ko Tsun Hsiung, one of the most popular actors in Southeast Asia, to play the male lead.

Spring Comes Not Again was my first experience making a Chinese film, and it turned out to be one of the most difficult films I have ever worked on. I speak Cantonese, the most common dialect in Hong Kong. However, most Chinese films are shot in Mandarin, the official spoken language in China and Taiwan, so I had to learn the dialogue phonetically. I was fortunate to work with the talented writer/director, Liu Fong Kong, who studied film in Italy. Despite the daily challenge of thinking in one language and "speaking" another, I loved everything about the people and the process.

What I *didn't* love was Hong Kong's Chinese gossip columnists, who surpassed Hedda and Luella in fabricating the who-what-where-when activities of major players in the movie business. According to the columns, I was either having an affair with my co-star (and everyone else on the set), or I was in a bitter fight with some of the other actors, and one of them was going to beat me up. There weren't enough hours in the day for me to have time for all those sexual escapades.

I didn't read the Chinese papers, but my stepmother did, and she faithfully reported what was printed every day. My poor father took it all so seriously and kept asking me what I could do to stop it. The answer was absolutely nothing. I learned that in Hollywood.

My poor father. On August 25, 1972, my stepmother called from the hospital and told me he passed away. When I arrived at the hospital, it was still dark outside. There were few people in the lobby. I went upstairs to my father's room, walked in, and saw his body suspended over the bed like he was floating in the air.

I stood there staring for a moment, then turned and rushed out of the room, trying to make sense of what I had just seen. I took a deep breath and went back into the room. This time, I saw my father lying on the bed. Aunty Nan was standing nearby.

I told my doctor what happened at the hospital, and he said I was in shock. I'd like to believe it was something more spiritual, something that can't be explained—that my father waited for me to come before he left this world.

For a long time after that, whenever I drove past the hospital, I felt an ache in my heart and tears in my eyes. Memories came back to me one by one.

I remember when we were children, my father would sing "You Are My Sunshine" and point at us, *his* sunshine. He had a good voice, and I always admired his singing in church, but sometimes we were embarrassed because he was always louder than the other church members.

When I was about sixteen years old and home for the summer holidays, I went out with boys at night. Every time I came home from a date, I took my shoes off to sneak upstairs to my bedroom so I could maneuver a couple of the squeaky stairs and not wake anyone, especially my father. Without fail, just when I thought I had made it up the stairs, my father would call me out. My punishment was a lecture on how to behave like a young lady.

I was still working on *Spring Comes Not Again* when I was in this fragile state, and one day, I had to act in a very emotional scene. It was the moment my character discovered that the love of her life had betrayed her and that he was leaving her forever. I thought I should burst out crying, collapse, and fall to the ground.

Instead, director Liu Fong Kong asked me to cry from within, to cry from the heart. It was a close-up, and if it came from the heart, he told me, the pain and loss would register on my face.

I thought of my father, remembered the real ache in my heart, and had no trouble doing the shot the way Liu Fong Kong wanted.

CHAPTER 16

On July 19, 1973, I had lunch with Bruce Lee and Raymond Chow. I noticed that something was off with Bruce, who was not his playful self. Instead, he seemed nervous, and when Raymond brought up the idea of our doing a film together, Bruce interrupted with complaints about his salary. It became so uncomfortable that I felt compelled to step in with the no-nonsense advice Bruce had come to expect from me. "You need to behave yourself," I told him, meaning that he shouldn't speak to Raymond so disrespectfully.

Then, I tackled the elephant in the room. People were gossiping about Bruce's relationship with actress Betty Ting Pei. What should have been a discreet affair (Bruce was no saint when it came to women) had become too public. He insisted it was just a fling, but I reminded him that by behaving indiscreetly, he wasn't being fair to his wife and children. His final words on the subject were that he loved his wife and had every intention of ending his affair with Betty.

I was concerned about Bruce, though, because he seemed so troubled.

The next day, I got a call from a friend, a member of the press, who told me Bruce was dead. I was stunned! I immediately said something like "Poor Linda and the children." My friend then delivered the second part of the tragic news. Bruce suffered his fatal cerebral edema while at Betty Ting Pei's place. I want to believe he went to see her to do the right thing.

Bruce's sudden passing at the incredibly young age of thirty-two was mourned universally, and he became a mythic figure and a cultural icon. Years later, in 1993, I was cast in the film *Dragon: The Bruce Lee Story*. I played Gussie Yang, the restaurant owner who encourages young Bruce to go to college and warns him that if he doesn't, he'll become a dishwasher. It was a case of art imitating life because Gussie's relationship with Bruce mirrored the one we shared for years.

I often thought of Bruce telling me he was going to be a big martial arts star and wondered what he would say about *his* life being the subject of a film. And now, over thirty years later, Ang Lee, the three-time Academy Award–winning director of *Crouching Tiger, Hidden Dragon*, *Brokeback Mountain*, and *The Life of Pi*, is preparing *Warrior*, another Bruce Lee biopic. Ang Lee described Bruce as a "bridge between East and West who introduced Chinese Kung Fu to the world."

Bruce was all of that, but I remember him as my wonderfully optimistic friend who, against all odds, shattered barriers on-screen and in life.

Not long after Bruce died, David Giler called with surprising news. *The Black Bird*, the screenplay he wrote when we were together, had been set up at Columbia Pictures by Ray Stark. David would direct, with George Segal starring as Sam Spade, Jr. I was so happy that David was getting his big break after the *Myra Breckenridge* debacle. Then, he made a very puzzling request. He said that Ray wanted me to come to Los Angeles to test for the female lead, the role David had written for *me*.

"Is he crazy?" I asked David, echoing my response when Ray called me all those years ago to offer me the part of Suzie Wong. But this time, I was incredulous about the idea of doing a test. Why would Ray, of all people, suggest that? He discovered me, gave me my first job, and knew my work better than anyone. I suspected he was playing some kind of game, but I couldn't figure out what it was.

Ray called me the following day to explain. Executives at Columbia (headed by David Begelman, who saved the studio from ruin in the early 1970s but destroyed himself after a notorious check forging scandal that led to his dismissal and suicide in 1995) had requested a test and insisted that David Giler direct it. Why? Because they were testing *David*, a first-time director, not me. Ray was setting up David for success by pairing him with an experienced actress who happened to be his ex-wife.

In truth, I loved the role and wanted things to work out for David, so I flew to Los Angeles and did the test.

Not long after I got back to Hong Kong, Ray called to say the studio liked what they saw, and the job was mine. There was one catch—the offer he made was well below my "quote," my salary for a lead role at the time. I told him to double the number.

Ray was a master negotiator who was used to getting what he wanted. I'm sure he thought I needed the job more than he needed me. *Poor Nancy—in Hong Kong and so far away from Hollywood.* He was surprised when I didn't jump at the chance to star in a studio film—and indignant when I asked for more money.

"I made you an offer," he snapped. "Take it or leave it." That was Ray being Ray.

I knew what I was worth, and it wasn't the ridiculously low amount he proposed. I turned down his offer, and that was that.

The role went to the French actress Stéphane Audran, who was probably very sorry she agreed to do it. I heard that David and Ray fought bitterly on the set. After the film was finished, David ran into his friend Warren Beatty and heard shocking news. "Hey, David," Warren said. "Do you know that Ray is reshooting the ending of your film?" David did not know because Ray didn't tell him, and since he didn't have final cut, there was nothing he could do when his film was ripped to pieces.

The Black Bird bombed at the box office and unfairly destroyed David's prospects as a director. It was impossible to fight with a Hollywood creature as powerful as Ray Stark and come out alive. That changed in 1979 when David unleashed a creature who was bigger and badder than Ray or any producer. David and his partners Walter Hill and Gordon Carroll produced *Alien,* a thriller about an existential monster on the loose in a spaceship. The film's terrifying tagline threatened, "In Space, No One Can Hear You Scream." The screaming in the audience, however, was heard everywhere in the world. *Alien* made over $100 million at the box office, and the film's sequels generated over a billion dollars.

And that wasn't all. In his parallel life as a screenwriter, David was responsible for a string of moneymakers, including *Fun with Dick and Jane, Southern Comfort, The Money Pit,* and *Beverly Hills Cop II.* David enjoyed a level of success that others could only imagine, but he also found peace. He moved to Bangkok and embraced Buddhism. Even though our marriage was a brief and maybe crazy interlude, we cared about each other and always remained friends up until his death in 2020.

I resisted Hollywood's siren call and stuck to my plan of raising Bernie in Hong Kong and making films that were close to home, especially when they were produced by Ross Hagen because he and his wife, Claire, were our extended family. In 1976, I went to Bangkok to star with Donald Pleasence in *Night Creature*, a thriller about a big game hunter with a grudge against a killer black panther.

On the first day of shooting, Ross introduced me to his friend, Norbert Meisel. They had offices in the same building in Los Angeles, and Norbert, who was also in the film business, stopped in Bangkok to visit the Hagens on his way to Tokyo. The next day, I was sitting with Jennifer Rhodes, the actress who played my sister in the film, when we spotted Norbert. "Let's save our per diem and let Norbert buy us dinner tonight," I suggested to her playfully. Jennifer looked doubtful because we had spoken to him for all of a minute. But I had a feeling. I looked directly at Norbert, who was talking to Ross, and smiled at him. He smiled back and, as I predicted, took us to dinner that very night.

I discovered that Norbert was a charming man—a great storyteller—with a fascinating biography. He had worked as an actor, a director of film and stage productions—he ran the Santa Monica Playhouse—and in his current job, he sold films internationally, which was why he was heading to Japan.

Most importantly, he was born in Vienna, which made him Austrian, like Max Schell and Peter Pock. I can't explain why Austrian men win me over at "hello," but historically, that seems to be the case. I suspect it has something to do with karma—that in a previous life, I had some unfinished business with Austria that I'm meant to complete in this lifetime. Who knows?

Norbert told me a story that suggested fate had some hand in bringing us together. In 1961, Norbert, who lived in Los Angeles, was walking on Sunset Boulevard, trying to cool off from a fight he had with his soon-to-be ex-wife. He stopped at an intersection and noticed a sports car idling at the traffic light. He recognized the driver as Max Schell, a fellow Austrian—but he was more intrigued by the beautiful young woman (his words) in the passenger seat. Who was she? The memory of that fleeting image stayed with him, and now, he realized it was *me*. Our paths had literally crossed in Hollywood, yet we were meeting for the first time in Bangkok.

By the time dinner was over, I had forgotten all about my mission to save my per diem. I was impressed by Norbert. He was sophisticated yet down-to-earth, knowledgeable yet inquisitive, and he seemed kind and generous. I was curious. What did he think of me? Would we see each other again? He called me from Tokyo, a little bashful but clearly interested in moving things along. Should he stop in Bangkok on his way home to California?, he asked tentatively. "Why don't you come back," I said, which I suspected was the answer he wanted to hear.

That one conversation launched so many intercontinental trips for Norbert—first to Bangkok, then back and forth to Hong Kong—that he jokes he's *still* paying off his credit card. Once we started seeing each other, we couldn't stop. Although the meeting that would determine if we had the possibility of a future together had yet to take place. I had to introduce Norbert to Bernie.

My son and I had built such a lovely life together. We grew up together, although he was such an old soul that I often felt that he was the teacher, and I was his pupil. When he was eight years old, he said to me, "Mom, you know there's so much suffering in the world." How does an eight-year-old know about suffering? We were a family of two, there for each other every day. I encouraged him to maintain a relationship with Peter and even sent him to Austria for a summer so he could get to know his father and grandparents. When he came home, he said he loved them and recognized that they had a place in his life, but he felt much closer to me. Bernie's opinion meant everything to me; as much as I cared for Norbert or felt that I *could* care, he would have to win my son's approval.

Norbert was very nervous about his impending meeting with my precocious thirteen-year-old. He came to our home in Hong Kong, uncertain of what to expect. Bernie immediately started talking to me about something he wanted to do, and we got into a discussion. Norbert offered his opinion, but Bernie wasn't interested in hearing it. He turned to Norbert and told him, "You know, this is none of your business."

Norbert apologized immediately. Bernie looked at him, sensing that his curt words had made Norbert feel uncomfortable and even a little sad. My son was deeply attuned to the feelings of others and never wanted to cause pain. "I'm sorry. I didn't mean to hurt your feelings," he told Norbert. Something clicked between them, an understanding that, with time, grew into mutual appreciation and genuine love. While Norbert was courting me romantically, he was also becoming the strong and supportive paternal figure who had been missing from Bernie's life. We fit together beautifully, and our long-distance family flourished.

At the age of thirty-seven, I felt that I was finally getting the life I wanted. I had a partner I respected and loved. Bernie was doing well in school and excelling at martial arts, a practice that became even more popular in Hong Kong after Bruce's death.

Then, my career took a dramatic turn later in 1977 when I announced the opening of Nancy Kwan Films (NKF), a state-of-the-art film production company headquartered in Hong Kong. After spending eighteen years in front of the camera, I felt completely capable of stepping behind it and running a company specializing in commercials, films, and television.

I had made films with some of the best actors, producers, directors, cinematographers, and technicians in the business, and I always paid close attention to how they worked. Actor Bill Holden knew his craft inside out. Producer Ross Hunter oversaw every single detail of his films. Cinematographer Geoffrey Unsworth always found the best way to shoot a scene. Being in their company and watching their process was better than attending film school. I benefited from years of on-the-job training and was eager to transition to a production role where I could use these skills.

My dream job came into focus when I started talking to Pearce Tong, who was the founder and owner of Hong Kong Recording Company and Empire Records, and the managing director of Pearce Commercial Studios, LTD. He had produced television commercials, recorded singers, and acted as creative director for a large advertising company. We both felt that Hong Kong needed a production facility that could work swiftly, professionally, artistically, and economically, unlike the existing companies whose technology was outdated.

Our plan to open a modern facility seemed like a pipe dream until we teamed up with investor Charles Wolnizer, the chairman and managing director of APA Leisure Time International, one of the largest film production companies in Australia. Wolnizer recognized the value of launching a company in Hong Kong and backed NKF.

We opened an office in a high-rise building in the Causeway Bay area of Hong Kong, taking over an entire floor. It was a great change for me in many ways and an exciting one. I went to the office every day, a new experience for me, and managed billings, budgets, proposals, and the productions themselves. I also had to master the proprietary technology that distinguished our company from the more established production facilities. We had one piece of equipment called the "rock and roll" that mixed dialogue, music, and background sound effects tracks simultaneously, enabling NKF to accomplish in a few hours what other studios took days to do.

We hit the ground running with a preproduction job for Paramount, a commercial for the Leo Burnett advertising agency, and a television pilot for CBS. I stepped behind the camera to direct and found so much of the process familiar. My muscle memory from all the times *I* was directed kicked in, and I knew where to place the camera and how to talk to the actors.

The biggest difference between commercials and feature films was the schedule. Commercials usually had to be completed in a day, so we had to move quickly, and there was no time for indecision or error. I remember casting a child for a candy commercial and then discovering that he wasn't up to the job. We didn't have time to ease him into the role. He had to be ready when the cameras rolled, but he wasn't, so we had to replace him, which was heartbreaking for the child.

Commercials also have a very focused agenda—to sell the hell out of a product, which means giving the actors very specific instructions. One of my associates showed me footage from a commercial made by another company featuring Orson Welles pitching a wine from Spain. It was surreal for me to watch the director tell Orson Welles—one of the greatest directors of all time—"Don't do it that way! Hold the bottle so we can see the label." But the director had to please the client—and Orson Welles had to listen to him because he was paid a lot of money to bring that vision to life.

I was happiest when my work was hands-on because I felt that I was learning and growing as a filmmaker. Unfortunately, the company needed me to cultivate new business. That role didn't appeal to me because I spent most of my time having lunch with clients to secure more jobs when I wanted to be out in the field directing and working in film production. I realized that being a managing director was not for me, so I resigned. My associates kept the company going for a while but eventually had to close it.

Meanwhile, Norbert tried to persuade me to move to California. Bernie thought it was a great idea because he wanted to attend college in the United States. I agreed that the change would be good, especially since Hong Kong's future was unpredictable. The city was prospering and had evolved into a thriving business center. Still, no one could predict what would happen when Great Britain's hundred-year lease ended in 1997 and Hong Kong would be returned to China. Even though the handover was eight years away, there was uncertainty. Some people came to Hong Kong hoping for a better life; others left to find a better life elsewhere.

The eight years that I spent in Hong Kong were precious because I had accomplished everything I set out to do. I spent time with my father, connected Bernie to his Hong Kong family and heritage, and proved to myself that I could manage my acting career and cultivate other talents and skills. I felt confident about my ability to create new opportunities in California. The bonus was Norbert. Whatever I decided to do in the future—act, direct, write, start a business—we would do it together.

CHAPTER 17

Bernie's reaction when we moved back to Los Angeles confirmed my feeling that it was the right thing to do. "Mom," he said, "I look like everyone else!" In Hong Kong, he was always the "other," the boy who looked different wherever he went. Now, for the first time in almost a decade, he was surrounded by light-haired, blue-eyed teenagers who shared his California, sun-kissed look.

Bernie may have looked Western, but he was Asian at his core. In some ways, he was more Chinese than I was. Starting at a young age, he learned Asian philosophy, poetry, and songs from his amah. We called him Little Buddha. Then, when we lived in Hong Kong, he took up martial arts and studied with his Sifu, a tai chi master, and eventually excelled in meditation, including Taoism and Buddhism. Bernie meditated for hours, and it opened a whole new world for him. He began to look within himself and became a very centered person. Unlike most teenagers, he never felt the need to experiment with alcohol or drugs. He had such a deep understanding of the connection between mind and body—and the importance of taking care of both—that I always thought of him as a spiritual warrior.

Bernie was also a wonderful teacher. He introduced me to tai chi chuan, an ancient form of exercise that promotes mental and physical harmony and wellness, improves balance, decreases the risk of high blood pressure, increases blood circulation, and so much more. We call it "moving meditation." Thanks to Bernie's instruction and encouragement—and my ballet training—I soon mastered the long form and practiced daily, which I continue to do today.

Bernie's new friends were so impressed by his cool martial arts skills that he started giving them lessons. Soon after we moved to LA, he decided he wanted to compete in a martial arts tournament and announced that he would enter as a black belt. "It's better to start at the top," he explained to Norbert. "I can always work my way down." Considering that Bernie was only sixteen, Norbert thought he was a little ambitious but volunteered to take him to the tournament. Bernie did brilliantly, winning second place, with first place going to a Japanese man in his early twenties (who congratulated Bernie and asked where he trained).

The next time Bernie competed he came home with the trophy for first place. I often wished my friend Bruce Lee was around to work out with him.

Bernie was always curious about how things worked and could master the most complicated machinery. When we bought him his first motorcycle, Norbert had to show him how to ride it, but in no time, he graduated to a massive Harley Davidson. Then, he started racing dirt bikes. Norbert accompanied him to the races and became his water boy and aide-de-camp, rushing to clean his goggles and fill his gas tank between laps. Bernie was so grateful for his help that he always handed him the medal he inevitably won. "It's yours, Norbie. You earned it," he'd say.

When he was older, he bought a 1954 pickup truck, took it apart piece by piece, and then rebuilt it so it worked perfectly. Then, he learned how to fly a plane.

He was also an artist. He painted, forged metal sculptures, created fanciful figures in paper-mache, and wrote poetry.

My son had so many talents, but what I admired the most about him was his kind and gentle heart. Late one night, Norbert went to the kitchen to raid the refrigerator and was startled by noises coming from the basement. Fearing that someone had broken in, he armed himself with a stick and opened the door. He was shocked to see a young boy wrapped up in a sleeping bag reading by candlelight. Norbert closed the door and ran to Bernie's room to get help. "There's a boy sleeping in the basement," he whispered. "Maybe we should call the police."

This was not news to Bernie, who explained how the intruder ended up in our basement. "He's a boy from France who has no place to stay, so I let him sleep here."

Norbert was shocked and even *more* surprised when Bernie confessed that the homeless boy had been living in the basement for three weeks. He didn't tell us because he was afraid of our reaction. We'd probably say no to the idea, and he knew that helping the boy was the right thing to do. How could we refuse our Good Samaritan? The desire to help others was built into Bernie's DNA, and we never wanted that to change. The boy stayed in the basement.

I was so proud of my son. Proud of who he was and proud of the man I knew he would become.

It took me a while to find my way back professionally in Hollywood. I had been away for so many years that I had to make new connections and remind people that I was still interested in working. But acting wasn't my only interest, especially after my experiences at Nancy Kwan Films. I wanted to write and produce, and I found a perfect creative partner in Norbert.

We developed a process that worked for us for decades. Whenever we got the urge to do a film, we'd turn to the actors, cinematographers, and friends in our orbit—Ross Hagen, Seymour Cassel, David Carradine—for help developing the script. Then we'd raise the money and make the film. Each project was a labor of love, a Mickey Rooney/Judy Garland "Let's put on a show" type of endeavor, with a dash of John Cassavetes's ingenuity. We did it for the joy of working, and miraculously, Norbert and I got through our projects without killing each other. Our one rule was that we *never* discussed work when we were at home.

The best part of taking time to ease into demanding acting jobs was that I could concentrate on building our new life. We bought a house, and Bernie and I became American citizens. We loved being a family, a novel situation for me because even when I was married to Peter, I was never home. Now, Bernie had a mother and a father in the same place at the same time. I'd hear Bernie, the fitness king, warn Norbert that he had to lose weight because "We don't want you to get sick. Mom and I need you," or watch them argue playfully over a game of chess. We spent so much time together that Norbert called us "the Three Musketeers."

I was so happy that I extended the family circle to include my mother. She had moved to Florida, and I called her regularly and made a point of going to see her on occasion. She had cancer, so her health was precarious, and while we still had unresolved issues about the past, I didn't dwell on them and accepted her for who she was. I didn't want to have any regrets when she was gone.

I invited her to visit us in Los Angeles. The first time she came, I arranged for my brother KK to be there because I thought it would be nice for her to meet his children, her grandsons. After spending a short time with them, she said, "Very noisy little boys, I think." Her reaction was *not* that of a typical grandmother.

But she *loved* Bernie. The second time she came, she got into a heated conversation with him about cars, and he offered to take her for a drive. She kept encouraging him to go faster— the steeper the hill, the better. "Faster, faster," she urged. Poor Nobert was sitting in the back seat, scared to death and holding on for dear life. That was Mother—she was a free spirit who did whatever she wanted with no apologies. When she passed away, I missed our weekly conversations.

Living in Los Angeles awakened so many memories of the different stages of my Hollywood life. I still had my old friends from *Flower Drum Song*. Reiko Sato and I had stayed in touch and saw each other occasionally. We hadn't gotten together for a while because she moved with Marlon Brando to his island, Tetiaroa, in French Polynesia. He planned to build a resort hotel there, so she told me she would be gone for a long time. I did not see Reiko again until after I moved back to Los Angeles, and she didn't say much about Tetiaroa, except that she was very disappointed because Marlon left her alone on the island for long periods of time.

Later, I heard a terrible story. Tetiaroa was essentially a deserted island. All supplies had to come by boat, and there was no way to communicate with the outside world. When Marlon left, he was supposed to arrange deliveries for Reiko, who was there alone, but he forgot. She was stranded on the island with a dwindling food supply and a terrifying rat infestation. She couldn't stand the isolation and the fear that something bad would happen to her. The next time a boat appeared, she escaped to Los Angeles.

I don't know what it is with my Asian actress friends. When we were young, most of them were either having an affair or recovering from an affair with Marlon. He had an insatiable appetite for Asian women. But what they saw in him...who knows? And, no, I never met Marlon Brando.

Not long after I saw Reiko, my friend, actress Nobu McCarthy, called me one morning and told me that Reiko was dead. At first, I couldn't believe it. I told Nobu that I had seen Reiko recently, and she looked fine. Nobu said that Marlon called Reiko a few times, but she never answered the phone. He went to her house to check on her and found her slumped on the floor, dead from a brain aneurysm.

Nobu, Norbert, and I attended Reiko's funeral at the Buddhist Temple in downtown Los Angeles. She was laid out in an open casket, surrounded by her family, friends, co-workers, and neighbors who had gathered to celebrate her life with sermons, eulogies, and chanting.

Finally, Marlon Brando stepped up to the podium and spoke emotionally about Reiko and their life together. At one point, he looked down at the casket and was so overcome with grief that he could barely get the words out. Suddenly, he reached across the casket with his left hand, pulled himself closer, and lifted his right leg, poised to crawl into the casket with Reiko.

Marlon was rather chubby, and Reiko was tiny. I held my breath, thinking, *Please don't try to climb into the casket, or worse, topple the casket and send it crashing to the floor!* I looked around and saw the same fear flash across the faces of the other mourners.

There was a tense silence as we waited for the worst to happen, then a collective sigh of relief when Marlon slowly (*so* slowly) took his hands off the casket, put his right foot back on the floor, and returned to join his family.

It was the most suspenseful moment I've ever experienced at a funeral.

I also tried to reconnect with Miyoshi Umeki, another friend from *Flower Drum Song*. Even after winning the Academy Award for Best Supporting Actress in *Sayonara* and making our film, she appeared in only a handful of other films. Miyoshi had a beautiful voice and often performed on television variety shows, but she was most visible as "Mrs. Livingston," the housekeeper in the television series *The Courtship of Eddie's Father*, a role that required her to speak pidgin English. Miyoshi wasn't happy about that, but when her son asked her why she agreed to speak in that demeaning way, she told him, "I didn't like doing it, but when someone pays you to do a job, you do the job, and you do your best."

Ironically, mild-mannered Miyoshi developed a reputation for being a tough negotiator on set. When she saw that Bill Bixby, the star of the series, had a trailer in a good location, she demanded the same treatment. She also advocated for casting Asian guest stars on the show, including Pat Morita and George Takai.

After the series ended in the early 1970s, and her husband passed away, Miyoshi retired, but first, she scratched her name off her Oscar statuette and threw it away, saying, "I know who I am, and I know what I did." She turned her back on Hollywood and moved to Missouri to be with her son and grandchildren.

Was she tired of working or tired of roles that ignored her talents and reduced her to a stereotype? I wonder. Over the years, I made several unsuccessful attempts to find her, and then I seren-dipitously met someone who said they knew Miyoshi and would try to connect us, but I never heard from her. I don't think she wanted to be found. I always hoped she was healthy and enjoying her life away from Hollywood. Years later, I heard that Miyoshi passed away in 2007.

1982 marked the start of my career renaissance. For the next few years, I worked steadily in episodic television and made-for-TV movies. I did not, as Ray Stark predicted, play "an Italian girl—or an American girl, a French girl, or an English girl." Most of the time, I was an Asian playing an Asian; Hoanh Anh in *Chicago Story*, Noriko Sakura in *The Last Ninja*, Dr. Lois Miyoshiro in *Trapper John, M.D.*, Anna Chen in *Partners in Crime*, Beverly Mikuriya in *Knots Landing*, Lily in *Blade in Hong Kong*, Lin Wu in *The A-Team*, Claudia Chen in *Noble House*.

In *Miracle Landing*, a drama about an airplane disaster, I was C. B. Lansing, the head flight attendant. No race was specified, but I did suffer a spectacular death early in the film when the fuselage cracked open mid-flight, and I was blown from the aircraft.

I was happy to work, and as Miyoshi said, "When someone pays you to do a job, you do the job, and you do your best." I took on projects for various reasons—because I liked the people or the subject, or I wanted to be in a certain place at a certain time. I'll say yes to almost anything that films in Hawaii because I love the location.

One of the earliest lessons I learned from Bill Holden, Glenn Ford, and other actors who came up through the studio system is that it is more important to work than to find reasons *not* to work. I always learn something when I do a film or a television show.

Whether it's an expensive NBC mini-series like *Noble House* or a small independent film like Norbert's *Walking the Edge*, I'm there to learn, grow, and hone my craft.

My willingness to accept the roles that were offered to me did not excuse the shameful reality that twenty-five years after *Flower Drum Song*, Asians still struggled to find meaningful representation in film. Casting wasn't the only—or even the primary—issue, although casting should be race blind. When I played the circus performer in *The Main Attraction*, the ingenue in *The Wild Affair*, or the oceanographer in *Fate Is the Hunter*, the character's race was irrelevant to the story, and that's the case in most films. A good actor can play anything. But on a parallel track, substantive roles had to be written for Asians so they would have opportunities and their stories could be told.

When actors ask me for advice, I tell them to be entrepreneurial and create their own material. One of the joys of working with Norbert on our homegrown films is that I can play any role. In *Walking the Edge*, I'm a female avenger who ruthlessly pursues the criminals who killed her husband. One reviewer wrote that I had come a long way from Suzie Wong and was now Clint Eastwood with a gun. I always appreciate a challenging role that has nothing to do with who I am in real life, and I loved the comparison to Clint Eastwood.

In the spirit of creating my own opportunities, I partnered with Norbert on a new project, and we included another show-business professional in our family—Bernie. When Bernie was still in high school, Ross Hagen brought his friend Erik Cord, an accomplished stuntman, to the house for a visit. Erik and I had worked together on the film *Wonder Woman*. That day, Erik saw Bernie do a backflip and then asked him to demonstrate martial arts moves. He was so impressed that he offered Bernie a job doing stunt work on the television movie *Murder Me, Murder You*, a pilot for the series *Mickey Spillane's Mike Hammer*.

Bernie literally jumped at the chance. The next day, he was in the wardrobe department at the studio being fitted for a dress and high heels so he could do stunts for the female lead. When they added the wig and makeup, he looked just like Brooke Shields—and I have the photo to prove it.

Once Bernie started working as a stuntman and actor, he never stopped. Walter Hill's *Streets of Fire*, *Police Academy II*, *Back to the Future*, *Real Genius*, *Teen Wolf*, and *Die Hard* were just a few of the movies he worked on in his early days as a stuntman. Directors loved him because he was unusually skilled, absolutely fearless, and completely professional. He performed dangerous stunts but never got hurt because he knew exactly what he was doing. Bernie had found the perfect profession, and he was very happy.

We decided to combine our love of tai chi with our movie-making skills to produce an instructional video, *Tai Chi Ch'uan* in 1984. Together, Bernie and I demonstrated movements, discussed the history of tai chi, and explained its benefits for the mind and the body. Bernie also demonstrated how tai chi could be used as a very effective self-defense aid. In one segment, we showed some of our celebrity friends, including John Saxon (who worked with Bruce Lee on *Enter the Dragon*), practicing tai chi moves with Bernie. We ended by combining thirteen lessons into a ballet-like dance called "Touching the Clouds." *New York Magazine* described it as "calming and beautiful to watch." The tape received a lot of publicity (including the television show where the interviewer accused me of making "everyone" think all Chinese women were prostitutes because I had played Suzie Wong). The tape was fun to do, and we actually made money.

Another business opportunity came my way when entrepreneur Frank Robinson asked me to do a commercial for Pearl Cream, a moisturizer from China that was made from pulverized pearls. It was the eighties, so everything in the commercial, from my curly hair and shoulder pads to my questionable use of the word "Oriental," looks and sounds wrong from a twenty-first-century perspective. But the ad was very persuasive at the time, so persuasive that we sold every jar and launched successful follow-up products. I know women who would give anything to get their hands on it today. Unfortunately, Pearl Cream lost its luster after Frank Robinson died, and the business wasn't the same without him.

We were busy! I was working on *Keys to Freedom*, a film about refugees fleeing Hong Kong before the handover to China, starring Jane Seymour and Omar Sharif. Norbert was in preproduction on *Night Children*, a project for me and David Carradine. And Bernie was weighing two job offers. He told me that he had to choose between a big-budget production and a smaller, independent film. For reasons of his own, he chose the little indie—*Far from Home*, starring Drew Barrymore.

CHAPTER 18

L adies and gentlemen, my fellow Asian Americans, I come to you this night, not as a Hollywood star...not as a motion picture actress. I come to you this night as an Asian American from Hong Kong. My name is Kwan Ka Shen."

The night was October 14, 1989, and I was in Washington, DC, addressing the Asian American Voter's Coalition at their fifth leadership conference. Earlier that year, the AAVC asked me if I would be their spokesperson and work with their group to encourage young Asian Americans to become involved in mainstream politics. I was very interested in helping them because I thought it was a call to action that would make a difference. Asian Americans should have a voice in shaping the government they embraced, and that would happen only when they voted, became involved in politics, and ran for office.

I labored over my speech, thinking about what I wanted to say and how I would say it. I introduced myself as Kwan Ka Shen because I wanted to emphasize that I was one of them—a Hong Kong native who had become an American citizen because I believed in my new country and all that it had to offer. I didn't talk about politics or parties. Instead, I said that we are people who have come far in search of a better life. We are Chinese, Vietnamese, Japanese, Philippine, Malaysian, Cambodian, Indian,

Thai, and from other countries that are known collectively as Asia. And while we will always have love in our hearts for our birthplaces, we treasure America because we know what it is *not* to be free. I stressed that freedom and opportunity come with responsibility and the need for respect, tolerance, and acceptance on both sides.

I was proud to deliver my speech to an appreciative audience and even prouder to be singled out by President George Bush for participating in the event when he addressed our group and promised to work with us.

Journalists often asked me how Asian actors were faring and if any progress had been made since my early days in Hollywood. Now, as a spokesperson for the AAVC, I could use a larger platform to bring recognition to Asian Americans and to help the Asian community beyond Hollywood.

I returned to Washington in 1990 when President Bush was scheduled to sign a proclamation officially establishing May as Asian/Pacific American Heritage Month. I had been selected as one of the honorees in a group of Asian and Pacific leaders from many walks of life, including architect I. M. Pei, Olympic Gold Medalist Sammy Lee, Miss Maryland 1989 Virginia Cha, Nobel Prize–winner for Physics Dr. T. D. Lee, and the first Asian American astronaut, Dr. Taylor Wang. I was proud to be in their company and wished my father could be with me to see where my long and eventful path from *The World of Suzie Wong* had taken me.

Understandably, I was a little nervous when I arrived at the White House and made my way to the Oval Office. In the distance,

I spied President Bush and his wife, Barbara, holding hands and laughing together, a reminder that they were real people, not just figureheads. Before the signing, I had a chance to tell I. M. Pei how much I admired his work and that my father had been an architect in Hong Kong. I also spotted a familiar face among the honored guests—Sammy Lee, whom I had met at a Los Angeles fundraiser for the East West Players Theater.

We stood behind President Bush during his speech and were proud to hear him say, "Asian and Pacific Americans are our fastest-growing minority population. They're changing America, and they are changing America for the better."

After President Bush signed the proclamation, he shook hands with us and gave me the pen he had used. I treasure it as a symbol of our progress and a reminder of the work that still needs to be done.

But I had another reason to be in Washington that May. I was working on *Endless Voyage*, an interracial love story about an American woman who is separated from her Vietnamese husband during the fall of Saigon. Writer/director Charles Wallace had asked me to play the United Nations delegate who attempts to reunite the couple and wanted me to work on the script and be involved as a producer.

We raised money to scout locations in Thailand and Vietnam, and after a trip to Hanoi, we secured hard-won government permission to film in Vietnam. This was a huge accomplishment because our project would be the first American movie shot in Vietnam since the fall of Saigon in 1975. I hoped that filming there would be another bridge to peace.

We were set to start filming in October 1990 but had to cancel the production because the money couldn't be secured. The sad reality of the film business is that many worthy projects never get made because of insufficient funds. It happens. Movies are expensive. I've learned to accept that I cannot always control a film's fate. But I believed in *Endless Voyage*, and I was sorry its important story would not be told.

While I was a spokesperson for the AAVC, a controversial issue affecting Asian American performers became headline news, and I was asked for my opinion. *Miss Saigon*, a blockbuster musical created by the team responsible for *Les Miserable* (and like *Endless Voyage*, a story about the dramatic consequences of the fall of Saigon), was moving from London to Broadway with its Olivier Award–winning cast: Lea Salonga in the role of the Madame Butterfly–like ingenue, "Kim," and acclaimed British actor Jonathan Pryce as the diabolical Eurasian known as "The Engineer."

Prominent members of the theatrical community protested Pryce's casting because he was white and wore prosthetics to alter the shape of his eyes. The protestors appealed to the Actors' Equity Association to block his visa, claiming that his performance was an insult to Asians and that an Asian actor should play the part. Actors' Equity complied with the request, prompting producer Cameron Macintosh to assert his artistic right to select a leading man by threatening to cancel the already sold-out show, a move that would eliminate the jobs of thirty-four Asian, Black, and Hispanic members of the cast (and everyone else associated with the production).

Who was right? Who was wrong? And, as Frank Rich wrote in the *New York Times*, could there even be a credible policy for "single-race exclusivity in the casting of some roles and complete racial freedom in the casting of others?" If a white actor were prevented from playing a Eurasian, would that mean Pearl Bailey couldn't play Dolly Levi? Or Denzel Washington Richard III? The situation was like the one that unfolded when David Carradine was cast as the star of *Kung Fu*. Was it worth it to dismantle an entire production over the appropriateness of one role when the show would provide dozens of roles for minorities?

I told reporters I could understand everyone's point of view and that it wasn't a simple matter of right and wrong. With the producer, it's an economic viewpoint—Pryce was a great actor and his star status would sell tickets. And from the Asians' standpoint, they're just saying, "Give us a chance"—the chance that they deserve to represent themselves. There should be a solution that could satisfy everyone.

Ultimately, Actors' Equity approved Pryce's visa. He played The Engineer and won the Tony later that year.

The *Miss Saigon* issue was complicated and messy, but it ignited a conversation about the importance of finding and creating opportunities for minority actors. I hope that one day, we won't look at people because of color or race but for their *abilities*. The best person should always get the job.

I got the job—a dream job, actually—when Vienna's English Theater, the oldest English language theater in Continental Europe, invited me to star opposite David Carradine in a production of A. R. Gurney's play *Love Letters*. The play presents two characters who tell their shared story by reading the cards and letters they've exchanged during their fifty-year epistolary relationship. Performing onstage—building a role in real-time as opposed to creating a character in disjointed scenes, the way films are made—enabled me to do something new as an actor.

Then I had the opportunity to appear onstage again, this time in San Francisco when I was cast in the Asian American

Theater Company's production of *Arthur and Leila*, a play about the fractious relationship between two Asian American siblings. Subsequently, the show moved to Los Angeles, where it was produced by the East West Players, a theater dedicated to promoting the works of Asian Pacific Americans.

The East West Players, founded in 1965, and the Asian American Theater Company, founded in 1975, were established to provide Asian American actors, playwrights, and theater professionals with a place to demonstrate (and refine) their talents at a time when they had limited representation onstage or in films. The show could be a contemporary play by an Asian American author or a classic—*A Chorus Line* or the *Fantasticks*, for example—featuring an all-Asian cast. In both cases, the actors, directors, and technical crew were given the opportunity to work in a theater where race was not a barrier.

Actors learn by playing all kinds of roles. If Asian Americans are denied the chance to play Juliet, Willy Lohman, Hedda Gabler, or Scrooge simply because they don't look the part, they're held back in immeasurable ways. The East West Players and other theaters with the same mission provide vital education and experience for these actors. In Los Angeles, over 75 percent of all Asian Pacific performers in the actors' unions have worked at East West Players. I'm proud to say I'm one of them.

These theater companies also foster new playwrights with the expectation that Asian American writers can tell stories that are meaningful to their community. Their mission aligns with the advice I always give young actors who ask how to build a career—I tell them to write their own material, to be their own storytellers. *Arthur and Leila* was written by Cherylene Lee, who played one of the children in *Flower Drum Song* when she was eight years old. She started out as an adorable child star and worked as an actress for years before she wrote her first play, *The Legacy Code*, and she later wrote *Carry the Tiger to the Mountain*, about the tragic life of a picture bride, and a memoir.

In *Arthur and Leila*, she masterfully explores the dynamic of sibling rivalry in an Asian American family. Dana Lee played my charming but dissolute brother while I played his well-intentioned but more conformist sister.

We lost Cherylene Lee too early—she died in 2016 before she could write more stories about Asian Americans and their quest for identity.

As busy as I was being an advocate, actress, writer, and producer, I knew in my heart that something was wrong at home. While working on *Far from Home*, the small film Bernie chose over the big-budget production, he started seeing Devora Fischa, the film's makeup artist, and their relationship progressed quickly. They moved in together soon after he brought her home to meet us. I expressed reservations because she was a little older than Bernie and much more worldly, but he felt differently. I told myself that my reaction was typical. Mothers are very protective of their children and don't always see the world as they do.

Coincidentally, disagreements between parents and their children were the subject of a film project I was offered. I was a fan of Amy Tan's bestselling novel *The Joy Luck Club*, the story of four Chinese women who came of age in pre-1949 China and their complicated relationships with their American-born daughters. In a more serious way, the book explored the generational divide portrayed in *Flower Drum Song*. And like *Flower Drum Song*, the book was poised to break ground by becoming a mainstream

Hollywood film with a predominantly Asian cast, which had not happened since 1961.

The producers sent me the screenplay and set up a meeting to discuss the role of one of the Chinese mothers. I read it and saw a line that disturbed me. In the script, one of the daughters is told by the mother of her Caucasian boyfriend that their relationship is a problem because of her race, which might stand in the way of his professional success. The daughter responds in an interior monologue, saying, "I couldn't believe what she was telling me. It was straight out of some awful racist movie like *The World of Suzie Wong*."

The novel includes an innocuous mention of "Suzie Wong" when a Chinese man looks at a woman and says, "I found you! Suzie Wong, girl of my dreams!" However, the reference in the script had a completely different meaning since the words "awful racist movie" preceded the title. In my opinion, *Suzie Wong* wasn't racist. And even if someone disagreed with my assessment of the film, there were a dozen other ways for the character to describe her feelings about the insensitive comments made by her boyfriend's mother. Using "Suzie Wong" as a slur promoted an unjust—and racist—stereotype.

I'd been fighting this battle for over thirty years, but I didn't expect it to come up on this project. I tried to explain my feelings to the producers, suggesting that the line didn't enhance the scene and was just an insult. I even wrote them a letter about it. They didn't see it my way and refused to take out the line.

My friends told me I was crazy to let one line stand in the way of a good role. I spoke to Ray Stark about it—our friendship had survived our heated negotiation about *The Black Bird*—and I knew he would understand my protective feelings about *Suzie*

Wong. He agreed that I should stand up for my principles. If it made me so unhappy to appear in a film that denigrated work that was meaningful to me, I should decline the role. I did, and I've never regretted my decision.

My problem with Bernie was not so easy to solve. The part that hurt was that we saw so little of him. Maybe that was normal, too, we thought. He was caught up in his first real romance and working constantly. He knew that Norbert and I were there if he needed us, and we understood that sometimes life gets in the way.

Our hope that everything was fine—and that eventually Bernie would find a way to balance romance and family—was shattered when he came to us and said that we had to talk about something important. He put his arms around me, started to cry, and then said, "I'm sorry. I've let you down."

I couldn't imagine why he would say that. Bernie never let me down. What did he mean?

"I'm HIV positive," he said.

I didn't know much about the science of HIV, the virus, or AIDS, the condition that it generally caused—no one knew much in these early days—but I understood that it was deadly, a modern-day plague. What my son was telling me didn't make sense. Bernie wasn't promiscuous, and he treated his body like a temple. He never smoked or drank alcohol. And he was lucky, blessed from the day he was born. He did stunt work for more than ten years and never got hurt. He raced dirt bikes, rock climbed, and surfed—all risky undertakings, yet he came through without any major mishaps.

He tried to explain. Devora had been diagnosed with AIDS. She'd had it for years but didn't know it and unwittingly transmitted it to him when they met. Now, she was very ill and in and out of the hospital. He didn't want to tell us, which is why he had grown so distant.

I won't try to describe my shock, sadness, and, yes, anger at the cruelty of fate because I didn't have the words then, and I don't have them now. Suddenly, a crisis that existed only in newspaper headlines was at the center of our lives. In 1992, there was no treatment or cure, just the terrible reality that, eventually, AIDS would take its toll.

If I had a magical machine or a wuxia superpower that enabled me to travel in time, I would go back to that seemingly ordinary day in 1988 to stop Bernie from making the fateful choice—one movie or the other—that led to this moment.

Like the flutter of a butterfly's wings that causes a hurricane thousands of miles away, his decision changed our lives forever.

CHAPTER 19

Bernie, the same Good Samaritan who sheltered a home-less boy in our basement, didn't think about himself. He was more concerned about Norbert and me. I challenged him, asking how he felt about Devora, knowing that he had this life-threatening disease. He still loved her and intended to take care of her. He even married her, "Because she needs me," he told us.

Then, my son asked me to help him. Devora was failing. He had to work and couldn't always be with her at the hospital. And if she was home, which she was on occasion, someone had to accompany her in the ambulance when she went to the doctor. Could he depend on me? I would do anything for Bernie, so I set aside my complicated feelings—my grief, anger, and disbelief—and did what he asked.

I sat with Devora and held her hand. I washed her face and made sure she was as comfortable as possible. I watched sadly as the young man in the room next door died alone because his parents wouldn't come to see him. No one should die alone, but ignorance about AIDS caused such fear and condemnation that many victims were abandoned by their families and friends. Bernie asked me to be better than that, and I tried...for my son. It took every ounce of strength I had and more.

Devora died in September 1992.

By that time, AIDS had become the number one cause of death for men in the United States between the ages of twenty-five and forty-four. I met with doctors to learn as much as I could about treatment, but they told me we were years away from effective HIV/AIDS drugs or a vaccine. Anticipating the worst, we asked Bernie to come live with us. He declined. If life was short, he wanted to make the most of it, and he had a plan.

Bernie viewed stunt work and his occasional acting jobs as transitional occupations. He envisioned becoming a screenwriter and director, and his attitude was, it's now or never. He was working on a script, *The Biker Poet*. He planned to direct and star in the film and wanted Norbert and me to produce it.

The Biker Poet was a tremendous gift of hope at a time when we had none. The project brought us together when we might have fallen apart. We embraced it wholeheartedly—to make Bernie happy and to give us a reason to get up every morning. It was as if everything we had done before *The Biker Poet* had prepared us for this moment. We knew how to make Bernie's dream come true—we financed the movie with money from the sales of the tai chi tape—and devoted our talents and resources to his film, our magnum opus.

The Biker Poet is best described as a gritty, modern-day fairy tale—*Alice in Wonderland* meets the *Odyssey*. A biker sets off through the new West on an episodic journey of self-discovery, rescuing a young girl from a kidnapper and encountering a wild variety of characters along the way. They show him that life is *never* what it seems. Enemies can be friends, dreams can be reality, and a quest can end exactly where it began because true enlightenment comes from within. Bernie wrote a magical story, profound, whimsical, and packed with clever references to film history, and we set out to bring it to life.

Bernie, of course, would play the biker. For the rest of the cast, we reached out to our extended family of actors, the friends we'd worked with over the years, and their friends, and they were eager to participate. Ross Hagen, who always enjoyed playing a villain, was perfect for the role of the kidnapper, and Claire Hagen played a waitress. Russ Tamblyn, who had starred in everything from *Tom Thumb* and *West Side Story* to David Lynch's *Twin Peaks*, became our Quentin Tarantino–inspired mob boss.

Bernie wrote a great role for Norbert, who played a cross between the Mad Hatter and the flamboyant emcee from *Cabaret* (very much like the role he played in real life) and he appeared in the film's dream sequences.

I played the Biker Poet's publisher, wearing a curly blonde wig because *why not?* When I asked Bernie why my role was so small, he promised to write a better one the next time.

The big question was, who would play "Deb," the precocious child Biker Bernie rescues from her kidnapper? Director Bernie spotted Amber Tamblyn, Russ's nine-year-old daughter. Amber was smart, poised, funny, and sassy. She held her own in every scene and, most importantly, never appeared to be acting.

Bernie had a good eye for talent. Amber grew up to be an accomplished actress who starred in *General Hospital, Two and a Half Men, Joan of Arcadia, House,* and other hit series. She also became a writer and credited Bernie, whom she viewed as a big brother, with being her inspiration because they bonded over their shared love of poetry. "He was the first guy ever who really got me to read my poems and be open about them. Bernie and I used to sit down together in between scenes and read poetry to each other," she said. When Amber published *Of the Dawn*, her first collection of poems, in 2000, she dedicated it to Bernie.

We shot the film in the high desert of Victorville, California, and at our friend David Carradine's ranch. Our resources were limited, so we had to be inventive. In addition to being the film's director, Bernie built and painted some of the sets, created all the artwork, and storyboarded every scene. I remember shooting a complicated scene that took much longer than expected. We were losing the light, so cinematographer Gary Graver drove his car to the set and turned on the headlights, our only source of light. We dealt with daily unforeseen problems, always managing to find clever solutions. Gary said it was his favorite way to work.

Every second day I had to drive to the lab in Burbank to deliver the footage we shot on location. An independent film producer is expected to perform multiple jobs, and this was the most demanding film I had ever worked on.

The set became a hangout for dear friends who wanted to help put on the show, including Bernie's fraternity of stuntmen who came to work with him on the car chases. "Anything for Bernie" was our unspoken motto. We put up with long hours and the heat in the high desert and raced to complete the film in three weeks, all so Bernie could do what he loved—surrounded by people who loved him.

The best part of making the film was that we could stop focusing on Bernie's health and concentrate on doing the job. We sweated over the budget and had disagreements like all filmmakers. I remember one heated discussion—in Chinese—about, of all things, a pot of soup. I argued that the camera would see that the pot was empty, while Bernie insisted the contents wouldn't be visible in the shot. The director always wins, and in this case, he was right. Bickering over small details felt wonderfully normal when our real-life issues were so big and the future uncertain.

When *The Biker Poet* was finished, we held a screening. Everybody loved the film. Bernie was so happy that he forgot about everything else and just lived in the moment. Soon after, he started to deteriorate. He moved in with us and expressed his pain and anguish in his art—his poetry, paintings, and intricate sculptures. In his "spiritual warrior" way, he prepared himself for the next world.

He departed for that world on June 5, 1996.

Shortly after Bernie was first diagnosed with the HIV virus, he dreamed he was climbing a sheer rock that led to a stone arch. The higher he climbed, the harder it got. The arch above him toppled, debris falling all around him. He made it to the top, but there was nowhere to go. Then, he heard me calling to him from a nearby ledge. I beckoned to him and threw a rope. He caught it and tried to swing across to me. He failed twice. On the third attempt, he landed next to me . . . safe.

That was only a dream. When Bernie fell, I could not save him. But he could save me.

Near the end, I was alone in a room at the hospital, meditating. Bernie was in his room, in a coma, and I was trying to reach him through meditation. Suddenly, I was startled by a series of loud knocking noises coming from outside the window. I looked at the window but saw nothing, so I continued with my meditation. After a while, the knocking sounds happened again. This time, I went to the widow, thinking it must be the wind or a bird hitting against the glass. I was on the fourth floor—there was no wind, no birds. Even though I couldn't see him, I knew it was my son.

Wherever I am, Bernie will always be with me. He was a wonderful son, my best friend, and my spiritual teacher. I will keep him in my heart forever.

I am a life
A force.
Always have been.
Always will be.

Bernhard Pock

CHAPTER 20

It's just not right for a child to die before a parent. I almost died myself and got to a point where I didn't care about anything and felt that I had nothing to lose.

I would go to sleep at night, but I didn't dream at all. This went on for about six months. And then I started to dream again. In the beginning, every time I dreamed about Bernie, he was a child. Then, Bernie started to grow up in my dreams, and after he grew up, I didn't dream about him again for a long time.

I wanted to create a memorial for Bernie and decided it should be a book about his short life, with his poetry, artwork, and the condolence messages I received from family and friends. Their recollections brought back so many memories of who he was and what he did at different stages of his life.

One friend recalled that when we moved back to Los Angeles, Bernie was so worried about crime that whenever we were together on the street, he carried an umbrella (in sunny California, where it rarely rained) so he could use it as a weapon if he had to protect me.

Ross Hagen wrote about the terrible jokes Bernie told us, usually when we were in the pool and a captive audience. Bernie got so excited that he always flubbed the punch line.

One of his young friends recalled that whenever she went hiking with Bernie, he could name all the animals, plants, and rocks they found along the way. He loved nature and felt at one with it.

In all the letters, the words that came up again and again were beauty, joy, love, and laughter, the essence of Bernie. Norbert and I published *Celebration of a Life* and donated the proceeds of the book and *The Biker Poet* to various AIDS foundations, hoping some good would come from our loss.

I drifted, trying to find my footing. Acting was always a welcome escape because I could disappear in a role. I was in Ross Hagen's movie *Murder on the Yellow Brick Road* and played Ming-Na Wen's mother on an episode of *ER*.

Around this time, I started visiting Ray Stark, who had suffered a debilitating stroke and was confined to a hospital-like room in his Bel Air mansion. Fran had passed away in 1992. After her death, Ray produced Neil Simon's *Lost in Yonkers* and a television production of *Barbarians at the Gate*, but in his later years, he functioned as more of an elder statesman in Hollywood. Now, he was a shadow of his former self.

The house, once the setting for spectacular parties, was quiet. Ray was attended by several nurses and his secretary, Janet, and his daughter, Wendy, was never far away, but I never ran into anyone else when I was there. Ray couldn't communicate anymore, so we sat together, watching television. He was in and out of the moment, but that didn't matter. We didn't need to speak. Our shared history was our enduring connection.

I thought back to a sad day in 1970, right after the Starks' twenty-five-year-old son, Peter, committed suicide. I paid a condolence call, and Ray walked me to my car when it was time for me to leave. Uncharacteristically, he got into the car and sat with me. He spoke haltingly about Peter; then all his emotions came pouring out—his disbelief, despair, and anger at the injustice of losing his child. I had never seen Ray this way, and his fragility touched me deeply.

Looking back, I understood exactly how he felt that day because I experienced the same emotions when I lost Bernie. We shared that bond, too. Whatever small differences we may have had in the past meant nothing. Ray was important to me, and I wanted to be there for him. When Ray died on January 17, 2004, a part of Hollywood died with him.

Later that year, I returned to the stage for a special reading of *Love Letters* to benefit the East West Players. My co-star was James Shigeta, and it was our first time acting together since *Flower Drum Song*. Although James worked steadily in television, he was not given the romantic male lead roles he deserved, not that any Asian actors were given those roles. As his agent predicted, James's future would have been much brighter if he were white.

But James had no regrets. "Playing heavies is always more fun," he said, referring to roles like Joe Takagi, the corporate executive in *Die Hard*, and Tim Yum Yum, the underworld crime boss in *Cage II: The Arena of Death*.

James was still his talented and charismatic self when we performed the play. We enjoyed working together and were heartened by the enthusiastic response from the audience. Our onstage reunion was a draw for Asian Americans who remembered our frothy scenes in *Flower Drum Song*. One couple flew in from New York to see the show, and a group in San Diego chartered a bus to Los Angeles.

Meanwhile, another fan of my early movies decided it was time to introduce my work to a new generation of filmgoers. Brian Jamieson produced featurettes and short documentaries at Warner Bros. He was very impressed by *The World of Suzie Wong* and *Flower Drum Song*—actually, he was a young fan of both movies when they first came out—and had the idea to release three of my lesser-known movies on a compilation DVD, with extra biographical material. Warner Bros. passed on the idea, but while working on the project, Brian became fascinated by my personal story and tried to figure out what he might do with it.

Simultaneously, Veronika Kwan Vandenberg, who was the head of international distribution at Warner Bros., asked if Brian could find a poster of *The World of Suzie Wong*. He had a few in his collection and brought them to her. Veronika was grateful and told him her aunt would be very pleased. "Who's your aunt?" Brian asked. When she answered, "Nancy Kwan," he was shocked. Kwan is a common last name, so he never made the connection that we were related. But now that he *knew* . . .

Veronika arranged for us to meet. After a three-hour lunch, Brian confided that he was retiring from Warner Bros.—*and* he wanted to make a documentary about my life.

"My life is not that interesting," I told him, dismissing the idea.

He looked at me and said, "I beg to differ."

After our lunch, Brian made it his mission to convince me that I was wrong.

His film credits were formidable. The documentaries he produced to accompany DVD releases included *Charlie: The Life and Art of Charlie Chaplin*; *James Dean: Forever Young*; and *Turning of the Earth: John Ford, John Wayne, and The Searchers*. He was knowledgeable about film history, involved in some important film restorations, and knew his way around archival material. He was also a master of promotion and publicity.

But what impressed me the most about Brian was his passion for this project. He came to our house almost every day to discuss the documentary and to win my trust. I'm a very private person, and I've never been comfortable talking about myself. But Brian was a skilled interviewer who knew which questions to ask, how far to probe, and when to stop. He was also a meticulous researcher who found long-forgotten photographs and newspaper interviews from the past. When he talked about my story, even *I* was interested because he connected it to film history and world events. Many of our conversations segued into an early dinner at a neighborhood pub, where we talked as we polished off a meal of fish and chips. Norbert and I became so used to having Brian around that trust stopped being an issue.

There was only one subject I was reluctant to discuss: Bernie. Brian wanted me to tell Bernie's story because he knew it was important, and he suggested there were thematic parallels between dramatic events in *The World of Suzie Wong* and my life.

In the novel and the film, Suzie has a baby—a son she loves dearly—who gets sick and dies tragically at the end. Remembering that Robert Lomax, her love interest in the film, told her he came to Hong Kong with a "To whom it may concern" letter of introduction to open doors for him in his new city, Suzie asks him to write the same kind of letter for her baby so that he will have an easier journey into the next world. It's a very touching scene in the film.

Brian wanted the deaths of our sons to be a life-imitates-art theme in the documentary and suggested calling the film *To*

Whom It May Concern: Ka Shen's Journey, referencing my birth name. While I appreciated Brian's artistic intentions, my feelings about Bernie were locked in my heart, and I couldn't imagine sharing them. Brian assured me that we wouldn't do anything that made me uncomfortable, so I decided to go ahead with the project, uncertain of where it might take me.

Brian was so committed to making the documentary that he planned to use his own money to finance half the budget. He reached out to investors for the rest, relying on his friends Sylvia and Ronald Young in Hawaii to help with fundraising.

Hawaii has always been a special place to me. The first time I set foot there, I was twenty years old and on my way to Hollywood. I smelled the sweet-scented air and thought, *Whoa! This is America? This is great!* I vowed I'd return, and I did as often as possible. In 2007, while we were setting up the documentary, Dr. Larry Tseu, Oahu's most popular dentist and a charming bon vivant, invited me to participate in a benefit sponsored by the Chinese Women's Club of Honolulu. I accepted happily, knowing my presence would help raise money for local charities.

It was a fortuitous trip because I bonded instantly with Larry Tseu, who was a wonderful host. With Larry as our guide, Norbert and I dined at some of Hawaii's finest restaurants and the trendy little places only insiders knew. Larry and I got along so well that we started calling each other pet names—he became "Dai Goh," which means big brother in Cantonese, and I was "Little Sis." Dai Goh proved to be more than a big brother when he heard that our documentary lost an important Hong Kong investor. Saying "We're family," he volunteered to provide the money we needed.

I was stunned by his incredible generosity. Thanks to Dai Goh, we were able to take advantage of a serendipitous opportunity to film a remarkable event, the premier of *Suzie Wong, the Ballet*, staged by the Hong Kong Ballet Company at Sha Tin Town Hall in Hong Kong.

I had to take a deep breath to appreciate the significance of this production. When we made *The World of Suzie Wong*, many people thought the story of a young prostitute who worked in a lowly Wai Chi bar perpetuated a racist stereotype that tainted the image of Chinese women—an idea that persisted for decades, even as recently as *The Joy Luck Club*. Now, forty-six years after the film sparked such controversy, Suzie's story would be the subject of a ballet, one of the highest art forms.

Norbert and I traveled to Hong Kong to attend the premiere of the ballet. Most of my siblings—KK and his wife, Moyra, Betty and her partner, Jeffrey, Annie and her husband, Charles, Teddy and his wife, Maggie—and some of my nieces and nephews joined us, making it a family affair. Brian and his crew filmed our arrival at the theater, including my reunion with Jackie Chan, one of Hong Kong's native sons and an international celebrity.

With his martial arts skills, easy charm, and comedic talents, Jackie joined Bruce Lee in the pantheon of action film stars with global influence. Hits like *Rush Hour*, more than 150 action and martial arts blockbusters, and video games have made him one of the most recognizable—and highly paid—actors in the world. His presence at the ballet signaled that it was an important cultural event.

We settled into our seats, the lights dimmed, and the ballet began. When I saw Suzie dressed in a red cheongsam, I was instantly transported back to 1960 and *my* Suzie Wong adventure. The performance awakened so many memories and emotions. As I watched principal ballerina Faye Leung dance, I saw my youth, *my* Suzie. I realized that *The World of Suzie Wong* was like a stone cast into the water. Its ripples carried me to many worlds and brought me back to Hong Kong, where I started. I had come full circle.

Where has the time gone? I thought.

There were eight hundred people in the audience that night, and they were captivated by the ballet and gave it a standing ovation. No one said, "Oh, she's a prostitute," or "Why did you make a ballet about a prostitute?"—reactions I often heard when the film came out, and long after. I saw their enthusiasm and acceptance and thought, *Well, well, well, we've come a long way.*

After the ballet, we continued our celebration at one of Hong Kong's famous night markets, where the neon buzzes and waiters at the restaurants practically throw plates at you—no napkins, no niceties, just delicious food, and it was wonderful.

While we were in Hong Kong, Brian interviewed my family and old friends. We also visited the Maryknoll Convent School, where I walked up the same staircase I *ran* up as a child. It was a sentimental moment for me to speak to the nuns, who wore conservative blazers and skirts instead of heavy black habits. They looked different, but the joyful spirit at the school was the same as when I studied there. I was introduced to a classroom of sweet-faced young girls who greeted me with smiles and a song.

Our next destination was Cambodia. Brian promised we would go to a special location for our conversations about Bernie. That place was Angkor Wat, a religious site that was dedicated to the Hindu god Vishnu when it was built and became an enormous Buddhist temple in the twelfth century. The existence of this sacred spot was threatened in the 1970s when Cambodia was controlled by the dictator Pol Pot and the Khmer Rouge. The country was given over to killing fields, where two million people were slain in a horrific genocide. Yet Angkor Wat endured.

I was nervous when we arrived at this historic place called the Eighth Wonder of the World because I knew it was time to talk about Bernie, and I wasn't sure I was ready. We walked through the ancient streets, awed by the massive statues and stone carvings. Then, children appeared out of nowhere and crowded around us, selling candy and souvenirs. Some of them spoke English. A young girl about ten years old told Norbert he could ask her to name any capital in the world, and if she answered correctly, would he give her a few dollars? Thinking he was clever and that she would never guess the answer, he asked if she knew the capital of Iceland. She came back instantly with "Reykjavik." Norbert was so impressed that he gave her ten dollars.

Later, I sat alone on a stone ledge, waiting for Brian and his crew to finish setting up the camera. I thought about that spirited little girl—Cambodia's new generation. I thought about the country's two million lost souls, whose presence I felt in this holy place. And I thought about Bernie, who fought so hard to stay alive but died at the age of thirty-three.

Instead of feeling depressed by these weighty thoughts, I felt that something was happening to me in this spiritual environment. I found strength. When the cameras rolled, I opened my heart and talked about Bernie's death in a way I never had before. I became so emotional that Brian wondered if he should stop filming. He didn't have to worry about me—as I spoke, I saw a path forward.

The days go on. The sun sets—the sun rises…Gradually, loss becomes a part of life…Now, I live in the moment…I don't plan very far ahead in the future or look back because it doesn't help to look back…I just live the best I can.

I still miss Bernie as much as the day he passed away, and the pain will always be there. But then Buddha says life is pain.

At Angkor Wat, I relived my life—the choices I made, the loss I experienced, the pain I carried. The experience was cathartic and liberating. I understood that death is a part of life.

And the greatest lesson of all—someday, even Angkor Wat will crumble and be a distant memory.

We are all just passing through.

EPILOGUE

The experience of making *To Whom It May Concern: Ka Shen's Journey* reminds me that we never know where a simple step forward will take us. Even though I had doubts when Brian Jamieson asked if he could make a documentary about my life, I said yes, which *changed* my life because I came out of it with more of a sense of purpose. I believed that others could learn from my stories, whether I spoke about my career or my personal life. My willingness to talk about Bernie could be meaningful to families who lost loved ones to AIDS, especially in the Asian community, where people tend to stoically repress their feelings—as I did—instead of expressing them. I hoped that hearing me speaking openly about AIDS might encourage them to do the same.

If I wanted my voice to be heard, there were many opportunities. In 2007, Arthur Dong interviewed me for his award-winning documentary, *Hollywood Chinese*, which provided an encyclopedic history of Asian Americans in Hollywood. His film was a worthy pursuit because it covered so much ground and established a record of the accomplishments—and struggles—of Asian American performers who worked, or attempted to work, in an industry that was indifferent, and at times hostile, to their talents.

Starting in 2008, I was recognized by several organizations:

the UCLA Asian American Studies Center; the Chinese Chamber of Commerce in Hawaii; the OCA (Organization of Chinese Americans), now known as the OCA-Asian Pacific American Advocates, which honored me with the Asian Pacific American Pioneer Award; and the Women's International Film & Television Showcase.

Then, *To Whom It May Concern: Ka Shen's Journey* was feted at several film festivals, including the Hawaii International Film Festival in 2010 when I received the Maverick Award and the San Diego Asian Film Festival, which presented me with their Lifetime Achievement Award.

It was heartening to be appreciated by a new generation of filmgoers because young people keep us young. Sometimes the most interesting questions came from festivalgoers who were seeing my films for the first time. What was Hollywood like then, they wanted to know. I realized that I had become somewhat of a historian. I experienced over fifty years of filmmaking and worked in all genres: an adaptation of a controversial bestseller; a big-budget musical; a love story set in the circus; a Mod romp; an anodyne sixties sex comedy; a Disney movie; a spy spoof; a suspense drama; a Chinese story of love and revenge; a bio-pic; several low budget thrillers; indie films; a documentary about Asians in Hollywood; and now *my* documentary. I had done it all, seen it all, and could offer my unique East–West perspective.

With all these accolades and lifetime honors, it seemed that my obituary would be next. But I wasn't finished yet! As much as I wanted to share my story and insights, I also wanted to have an impact. What could I do today that would be meaningful tomorrow?

For one thing, I could teach. Cal State, a public university in Los Angeles, has an acting program that prepares students for careers in film, television, and on the stage. The university approached me about teaching an advanced seminar to graduate students. Even though I had never taught before, I know a lot about acting and thought it would be interesting to share what I've learned with actors starting their careers.

My approach may have been a little unorthodox—I had my students, who were brilliant and percolating with ideas about films and filmmaking, meditate at the beginning of each class to calm their thoughts. I think the most valuable lesson I taught them was to be confident—believe in yourself—because that feeling is the foundation of anything an actor hopes to accomplish onstage or on-screen. Whenever they performed scenes in class, I would point out any behavior that didn't sound real and encourage them to be true to themselves. "If you don't believe in what you're doing," I'd tell them, "no one else will." Sometimes the simplest advice is the most powerful. I enjoyed teaching and learned as much from my students as they did from me.

Although several years had passed since my trip to Cambodia, I couldn't stop thinking about the children I met at Angkor Wat and wondering how I could help them. The idea I kept coming back to was to organize a charity event to raise badly needed funds for an orphanage in Siem Reap. I had heard about the orphanage when we were filming in Angkor Wat, but I didn't have a chance to go there. I knew how difficult it would be to cut through the red tape and connect with the right people in Cambodia, but our dear friend Sylvia, who was with us when we made the documentary, discovered a way for me to realize my dream.

She told me about AmaWaterways, a company that operated river cruises in destinations all over the world. Usually, they're pleasure trips, "Tulip Time in the Netherlands" or "Christmas Markets on the Danube." But many of the passengers who took a cruise called "Vietnam, Cambodia, and the Riches of the Mekong," especially the ones who went to Angkor Wat, were touched by the plight of the local children and, like me, wanted to help them.

In 2011, AmaWaterways announced that the company would co-sponsor a new school in the province of Siem Reap in Cambodia. Working with the Orphans and Disabled Arts Association (ODA), they co-sponsored the ODA Free Village School, which provided children with the opportunity to learn English and develop their skills as artists—invaluable tools that would improve their lives.

Passengers on the company's Cambodia cruise were invited to meet and interact with the children at the school and orphanage. I was touched to learn that many of them were orphaned when their parents died from HIV/AIDs or from land mines. This was the opportunity I had been searching for—a return trip to Cambodia that could address the needs of the children.

Sylvia, Brian Jamieson, and I invited our relatives and friends to join us on the cruise, and in no time, we assembled a formidable group of fifty, including my brother KK and his wife, Moyra; my sister Betty and her partner, Jeffrey; some of our friends, Cecil, Adele and her husband, Bruce; and even Takayo from my tai chi class and her daughter Juliet. We stayed in Siem Reap for three days, spending time with the children at their school and at the orphanage where they lived.

On the last night of our trip, we invited thirty of them to come to our hotel for a special fundraiser featuring raffle tickets, movie posters, and artwork created by the children. The most popular items were postcards with images of the children's impressionistic paintings and drawings, which sold out immediately. Everyone who attended was very generous, and by the end of the evening, we had raised $10,000 for the orphanage, money that would go a long way to buy art supplies and computers.

The three days we spent in Siem Reap and our visit to the English Language School and Orphanage were highlights of my life because I felt we had made a real difference.

I participated in two programs that had great educational impact. The New-York Historical Society invited me to speak in conjunction with their exhibition, *Chinese Americans: Exclusion/ Inclusion*. The exhibition explored the history between China and the United States and posed the question, "What does it mean to be an American?" I was fascinated by images of Cantonese opera houses in New York's Chinatown, where traveling troupes performed for immigrants who missed the entertainment they had enjoyed in their homeland. Bruce Lee's father acted in one of those troupes in San Francisco.

Another significant period in history was on display at the Chinese Railroad Workers Memorial Project in San Francisco when, in 2015, I was honored with a Lifetime Achievement Award. The railroad workers were America's unsung heroes. Separated from their families by cruel legislation and forced to endure harsh working conditions for little recompense, these men built the railroads, the backbone of the country's prosperity. It's easy to get caught up in the story of Asian Americans in Hollywood because the glamorous setting is tantalizing, but the stories of these unnamed and unappreciated railroad workers are sobering and humbling.

I'm often asked how anti-Asian prejudice has changed—and how it hasn't—in my lifetime. The best antidote to prejudice is pride, the pride that comes with celebrating the remarkable history of Asian Americans. I'm happy to add my voice to that constellation. I've lived through empowering highs and terrifying lows. I've been told that I'm "too Asian" or "not Asian enough," when, in fact, I'm just right. I know that positive stories can effect change, and I hope that these words, the story of an imperfect life, but one I have lived fully and authentically, can reinforce that important message.

In the end, that's the true American Dream.

AFTERWORD

*O*ne day Bernie said to me, "Mom, you know we are not from here."

I looked at him.

"We are stardust from other planets," he continued. "We came here to start a new world, and when our journey is completed here on earth, maybe then we go back to our origin."

I nodded in agreement.

NANCY'S SPEECH

I do not plan to talk tonight about politics or parties, the left or the right or center.

I want to talk for a moment about who we Asian Americans are and where we have come from. I plan to speak for a moment to the Americans who have opened their hearts and their country to our people. And I have a few words for our fellow Asian Americans.

Who are we and where do we come from? We are people who have come far in search of a better life. We are Chinese, Vietnamese, Japanese, Philippine, Malaysian, Cambodian, Indian, Thai, and from other countries known collectively as Asia. We have endured war and peace, governments and dictators. We have suffered from typhoons, monsoons, floods, and yes, from bullets and bombs. We are people who love, marry, and have children. We want our young ones to have a better life than we have known.

We are people who know laughter and tears and joy and happiness. We also know the sadness that comes from great hurt.

We are people with dignity who treasure family. We work hard and want to learn more and better our families—for our children and for our country that is now America. We have a tenderness for simple things and a love for flowers, music, poetry, and art. As we have had great patience for the past, we have great faith in the future.

We come from a world that has had a civilization for many centuries. We have had kings, emperors, presidents, dynasties, and ruling bodies. We are people who respect authority. We understand bureaucracy, procedure, and government.

We know right from wrong, good from bad. We know the difference between yesterday and today and tomorrow. We have hopes and dreams and always our family, our family. Our family. This tradition of family is the cornerstone of our world.

What is new for us is the understanding that we can have the freedom to love, to live, to reach out, and know that we are free to learn everything that can make us a better people with opportunities that are unlimited. What is overwhelming for us is that everything is here for us to experience, to touch, to see, to hear, to read about, to talk about, and to be a part of.

To the Americans, who have been so generous as always with their country, we want to say we are old from our world, older than you in many ways. And you are giving us something precious, that we have not always known—the energy of a young country and for us to be young again. You are giving us the opportunity to be American and to be free. Please give us time to catch our breath. Many of us come from refugee camps where we had been penned up for years with no hope and few dreams. Many of us come from places where our work was a way to survive, not a way to grow and achieve. Others come from places where, for years, no one has even asked us our name.

And please understand that we do not forget our ancestors, and our country and our homes, just as you have had times in your life for which you have warm memories. We will always have love in our hearts for our birthplaces.

As Asian Americans, we want to be good Americans. We are gathered here tonight to celebrate a unification that can help us. We want to vote and we will vote. We cherish the thought that we can make a difference—that we can have an opinion—and that we can believe in something and not be punished because as human beings we can think.

Here this night, people from almost every country in Asia are represented, as are many people from our new America.

We will honor your government and your history and your ways. We will be a part of your schools and your universities and your workplaces. We will help others and we will help our own people. Be what your country stands for throughout the world. We treasure what you are for. We know, perhaps even more than you do sometimes, what the word "freedom" really means. We know what it is not to be free.

To those who are still where we came from, we wish better times. To the Asian Americans who are here and are coming here every day, we say welcome to the American people. We say have patience. We are old in our ways, but young in yours.

I pledge to you that I, Kwan Ka Shen, will do more to be better as a free human being. I want to thank you for my heart. I want to smile at you and touch you and let you know that we are grateful that you have given us love, life, and freedom. The people in this room will pledge the same, and they are gathered here to do just that. To guide, to encourage, to inform, to set an example for all Asian Americans who express the joy to be in this great country.

ACKNOWLEDGMENTS

I want to express my deepest appreciation to my family and friends for their generous contributions and support. The journey began with Kevin Kwan, my second cousin thrice removed, who encouraged me to take the first step in writing my memoir and also penned the eloquent foreword to this book.

Deborah Davis is the best collaborator anyone can wish for—her inspiration and guidance have been invaluable.

My thanks to Veronika Kwan Vandenberg, Brian Jamieson, Dr. Lawrence Tseu, Dai Goh, Debbie Jiang, Wendy Stark, Janet Garrison, David Tadman, Cecil Tang, Adele Yoshioka, and Arthur Dong.

I appreciate the support and enthusiasm of my loyal fans, Cindy Yee, Lina and Mark Longtin, and Nicholas Kierniesky. I'd also like to acknowledge my friend and fellow actor, Dana Lee, and Noel DeSouza, my oldest friend in Hollywood.

I would also like to thank my agents, Larry Metzger and Susan Canavan, and my attorney, Arnold P. Peter.

As always, I am grateful to my family—KK and Moyra, Betty and Jeffrey, Annie and Charles, and Teddy and Maggie.

And thank you, Norbert, my partner, and Bernie, my spirit guide, for inspiring me every day.